T0035748

MACHIAVELLI

ALSO BY PATRICK BOUCHERON

France in the World (editor)

The Power of Images: Siena, 1338

MACHIAVELLI

THE ART OF TEACHING PEOPLE WHAT TO FEAR

PATRICK BOUCHERON

TRANSLATED FROM THE FRENCH BY
WILLARD WOOD

Other Press
New York

Originally published in French as *Un été avec Machiavel*
in 2017 by Éditions des Équateurs, Paris.
Copyright © Éditions des Équateurs / France Inter, 2017
English translation copyright © Willard Wood, 2018

Production editor: Yvonne E. Cárdenas
Text designer: Julie Fry
This book was set in Dante and Nobel.

6th Printing

All rights reserved. No part of this publication may be reproduced or transmit-
ted in any form or by any means, electronic or mechanical, including photo-
copying, recording, or by any information storage and retrieval system, without
written permission from Other Press LLC, except in the case of brief quotations
in reviews for inclusion in a magazine, newspaper, or broadcast. Printed in the
United States of America on acid-free paper. For information write to Other Press
LLC, 267 Fifth Avenue, 6th Floor, New York, NY 10016. Or visit our Web site:
www.otherpress.com

Library of Congress Cataloging-in-Publication Data
Names: Boucheron, Patrick, author. | Wood, Willard, translator.
Title: Machiavelli : the man who taught the people what they have to fear /
    Patrick Boucheron ; translated from the French by Willard Wood.
Other titles: Un Été avec Machiavel. English
Description: New York : Other Press, 2020. | "Originally published in French
    as Un été avec Machiavel in 2017 by Éditions des Équateurs, Paris.
    Copyright © Éditions des Équateurs / France Inter, 2017
    English translation copyright © Willard Wood, 2018" — T.p. verso. |
    Includes bibliographical references.
Identifiers: LCCN 2019025723 (print) | LCCN 2019025724 (ebook) | ISBN 9781590519523
    (hardcover : acid-free paper) | ISBN 9781590519530 (ebook)
Subjects: LCSH: Machiavelli, Niccolò, 1469–1527. | Machiavelli, Niccolò,
    1469–1527 — Criticism and interpretation. | Political scientists — Biography. |
    Political ethics. | Political science — Italy.
Classification: LCC JC143.M4 B6413 2020 (print) | LCC JC143.M4 (ebook) |
    DDC 320.1092 — dc23
LC record available at https://lccn.loc.gov/2019025723
LC ebook record available at https://lccn.loc.gov/2019025724

CONTENTS

POLITICS OF WRITING

REPUBLIC OF DISAGREEMENTS

NEVER TOO LATE

MACHIAVELLI

Cover of *Time* magazine, February/March 2017

THE ART OF TEACHING PEOPLE WHAT TO FEAR

"REAL POWER IS — I don't even want to use the word — fear." This sentence could have been written by Niccolò Machiavelli. It was spoken by Donald Trump in March 2016 when Trump was still only a candidate for the U.S. presidency, and these words now appear as the epigraph to Bob Woodward's book *Fear: Trump in the White House*. Is a more off-putting introduction to our subject imaginable? If we are tempted to assign words spoken by Donald Trump to Machiavelli, it's not just because many Western leaders have, and for a long time, bolstered their sense of their own power by affecting a cynical and crafty tone in the belief that it represents the last word in Machiavellian thought. It's because *we literally don't know what to think of Machiavelli*. Should we admire him or not, is he with us or against us, and is he still our contemporary or is what he says ancient history? This little book doesn't pretend to resolve these questions; nor is it

1

addressed to those who will read it to feel that they have right on their side — whether that side is answerable to justice or to power. On the contrary, this book tries to stay in that uncomfortable zone of thought that sees its own indeterminacy as the very locus of politics.

I should, at this stage, give a few explanations about this book — who is speaking, and to whom. I don't consider myself a historian of political ideas, but I approached Machiavelli a decade ago, yoking him with Leonardo da Vinci in an essay on contemporaneousness. Unexpectedly, I found Machiavelli a useful guide and support — I'd almost say a faithful friend, one whose intelligence never failed me. This might seem overly sentimental if it didn't echo Machiavelli's own image of discoursing with the ancient Greeks, as he put it in his famous letter to Francesco Vettori in 1513, where he describes writing *The Prince*: "I am not ashamed to converse with them and ask them for the reasons for their actions. And they in their full humanity answer me."

My conversations with Machiavelli became more regular and fruitful as I approached topics of which the Florentine author was, in his day, the most clear-sighted analyst. This happened first as I researched the political meaning of the architecture of the quattrocento. Machiavelli taught me to see it less as a representation of power than as a machine for producing political emotions: persuasion, in the public buildings of the republican city-states; and intimidation, in the fortified stongholds that the princes built to keep those states in line. It happened

2

again when I was trying to understand how the political instability of Renaissance Italy, riven with conspiracies and coups d'état, represented a structural element of princely power, which inevitably uses violence as the foundation of law. In every case, Machiavelli proved a worthy brother-in-arms who, because he had thrown light on his own times, threw light on ours — proving himself a contemporary in the very best sense.

During the summer of 2016, I gave a series of daily talks on French public radio in which I tried to articulate this capacity of Machiavellian thought to sharpen our understanding of the present. This little book collects those texts, which in their biting brevity and direct address attempt to harmonize in *style* with Machiavelli — not simply his manner of writing but his art of thinking, which brings to a flash point the fusion of poetry and politics.

Only one of these talks was not broadcast on the France Inter network during the summer of 2016, the fifth, focused on Machiavelli's reading of Lucretius's *De natura rerum*, "a dangerous and deviant book that makes the world jump its rails and come off its hinges." The plan was to air the episode on Friday, July 15, but it was swallowed up by the sorrow, anger, and numbness that followed the terrorist attack on the Promenade des Anglais in Nice on July 14, France's national holiday, when eighty-six people were killed and more than four hundred wounded. Although this book restores the text to its original place, there is still a gap left by the lasting stamp of fear.

Is that why I have chosen to give prominence in the book's American edition to the politics of fear? Not solely. As I write this preface, I am remembering a dialogue that I had with the political scientist Corey Robin, the author of a major book in 2004, *Fear: The History of a Political Idea*. "One day," he wrote, "the war on terrorism will come to an end. All wars do. And when it does, we will find ourselves still living in fear: not of terrorism or radical Islam, but of the domestic rulers that fear has left behind." Our discussion, which led to the publication in 2015 of *L'exercice de la peur: usages politiques d'une émotion* (Spreading fear: the political uses of an emotion), asked whether the American way of fear might be exported around the world. We touched on Hobbes, of course, de Tocqueville and Hannah Arendt, but also Machiavelli, who continually inquired about the fears of those who govern: What makes them truly afraid? When justice stops being effective (or when crimes of corruption stop being punished) and when political violence is no longer a threat, there is nothing left to cause fear in those who govern shamelessly, that is, buoyed by a mood they aren't in control of and that no one is on hand to countervail. What will then happen to the republic? This question inevitably arises when anxiety is felt about democracy, because the republic loses its stability when it no longer reflects a pacified equilibrium between the different fears that divide it.

In 1975, J. G. A. Pocock defined that loss of equilibrium as "the Machiavellian moment," when there is daylight between a republic and its values. American historians have since associated Machiavelli's name with that form of political crisis, a practice I have followed in this book. And today we are undeniably living through another Machiavellian moment, again bringing the Florentine author close to the core of American reality. But the author of the present lines is in no position to analyze the ins and outs of the situation, other than by this cross-Atlantic dialogue. What is fundamentally at stake is the capacity of the available political language to make sense of current developments.

Living in unstable times, Machiavelli was keenly aware that the old political lexicon, which the Middle Ages had inherited from Aristotle, no longer served him adequately. One instance was the basic opposition between the ideas of reigning and dominating, which lay at the heart of the medieval concept of government (the *regimen*). By describing the exercise of power as a skilled technique of domination, Machiavelli showed that the old political language, founded on key distinctions, was out of date. And Machiavelli defined the intellectual's task as a kind of resoluteness toward truth — being unmoved by the dazzle of words to "go straight toward the actual truth of the matter" (*andare drieto alla verità effetuale della cosa*). This experience, which is profoundly Machiavellian in nature, is one that recurs again and again in history, whenever the words for expressing the things of politics become obsolete. What do we do when confronting adversaries we can't put a name to? We call

5

them "fascists," for want of a better term — just as in Italy's medieval communes, the people called the lords "tyrants." We intend to confound them, to abash and bring them down, when we should in fact be examining what they say closely for its fascist potential. One thing is certain: when we use words from the past, we are showing our inability to understand the present.

Since the summer of 2016, in France but also in the United States and elsewhere, every political forecast has been systematically proven wrong. In the past few years it seems that the perverse pleasure that the public takes in contradicting pollsters — who minimize the voters' ability to choose by presenting developments as foreordained — has turned to fierce vindictiveness. Looking only at electoral results, from the United Kingdom's Brexit vote on June 23, 2016, on whether to remain in the European Union, to Donald Trump's election to the U.S. presidency on November 8 of that same year, the *qualità dei tempi* has definitely turned to storms. The consequences for the French electoral cycle, starting in January 2017, were similarly astounding. Following a series of extraordinary circumstances that eliminated all the expected candidates one after another — those picked either as favorites or as dead certainties — the election gave the presidency to Emmanuel Macron, a man who happened in his philosophical youth to have written an essay on Machiavelli. When a journalist asked me about this electoral smash-and-grab, so characteristic of the boldness commended by the author of *The Prince*, I glibly described Macron as a "Machiavelli in reverse," meaning that the French president had abandoned philosophy for politics, whereas Machiavelli chose to make his mark in philosophy when politics abandoned him.

What import does a virtuoso of political ruses like Machiavelli have for us? If he were nothing more than the wily and unscrupulous strategist that a hostile posterity has portrayed him to be, then not much at all. In these troubled times, when the stutterers can't be told from those who are talking of the future, the last people anyone wants to hear from are the so-called experts at predicting trends, who reduce all the indeterminacy in political life to a few elementary rules of collective action. The simplicity of those rules has everything to do with the experts' lack of imagination.

Machiavelli is that thinker of alternatives who dissects every situation into an "either/or," drawing a crossroads of meaning at every stage of historical development. But if he is captivating, it's because he lets us see how the social energy of political configurations always spills out of the neat constructs in which it's meant to stay put. His sentences invariably run away with him; he has no sooner declared that there are only two avenues than he proceeds down a third. When we try to work out whether a particular political situation is going to turn out one way or another, it's well to remember that it is carried along by a general movement that has already occurred. Perhaps this is what awaits many European and other world nations: they are so worried about a pending catastrophe that they won't understand when it has already happened.

People who see history as primarily tragic have always felt that the scenes of our disarray might well have been penned by a ghostly Shakespeare. But as "the grotesque wheels of power" (in Michel Foucault's phrase) grind into motion, it seems that the coarsening of public discourse we are now experiencing got its start on a less exalted stage — none other than that misleadingly named feature of Trumpian America known as "reality TV." It is there that a general disregard for the "actual truth of the matter" (to speak in Machiavellian terms) was patiently nurtured. Not for the first time have upcoming politics had their start in fiction.

That's why, in 2017, there was such a surge of interest in the United States in George Orwell's *1984*. Literature doesn't predict the future any more than it protects us from its threats. It warns, yes, in the sense that it sounds the alert about a catastrophe that generally doesn't happen, or not in the way it was imagined. Ever since 1984 came and went without bearing out Orwell's dystopian predictions, we no longer read his novel as a foreshadowing or preview of a totalitarian regime. At this stage, we know that totalitarianism is a category not so much meant to describe a political reality as to make that reality fit into a preestablished form — for instance, at the end of World War II, when the liberal democracies were intent on demonstrating that Communism would pursue Nazism by other means.

In a sense, totalitarianism is a political fiction. It had its first trial in George Orwell's 1949 fable and was then given a theoretical analysis by Hannah Arendt in 1951. We now know that what came after, what obtains today, took its place without receiving a name. Orwell imagined the tyranny of a "Ministry of Truth," but that's not what happened, and we don't yet know if it's for better or worse. "The Party told you to reject the evidence of your eyes and ears," Orwell's hero, Winston Smith, says in 1984. And: "Not merely the validity of experience, but the very existence of external reality was tacitly denied." What the novel describes is the capacity of propaganda to hollow out a receptive space in people by undermining reality and sense experiences. "The evidence of one's eyes and ears" referred to by Orwell could be common sense; it could also be that sixth sense Machiavelli spoke of, the accessory knowledge that the people have of what is dominating them.

Admittedly it was not the Party, as imagined by anti-totalitarian writers, that spoke when Sean Spicer, the White House press secretary, declared, "Our intention is never to lie to you," before adding "sometimes we can disagree with the facts." It's not a Party, but it's something else that we don't know what to call, a fiction that is taking on body under our eyes. And what we need to understand is: What is this taking on of body, and how can our own society come to embody monstrousness? Gramsci read Machiavelli's *The Prince* replacing the word "prince" with the word "party." We could in turn read

Orwell and replace "party" with "prince." Either way, Machiavelli needs to be read not in the present, but in the future tense.

We don't know today which Machiavellian fictions hold the resources of intelligibility that will open our future to us. Is it the philosophy of necessity expounded in *The Prince* and that illusionless treatise on republicanism the *Discourses*? Should we look in Machiavelli's work for the art of coming to terms over our disagreements or look instead for that skill the dominated have of recognizing the science of their domination? And in that case, why not look at his theater, his histories, even his love poetry? I tried during the summer of 2016 to reconstruct the face of Machiavelli hidden by the mask of Machiavellianism; and if that face turned out to be as changeable as a storm-tossed sky, it's because its owner hardly had the time to choose among his different talents. They all brought him back to his art of naming with precision that which was happening, his ability to take stock implacably, inextricably joining poetry and politics.

Three years later, what is the sense of spending further time with Machiavelli? The same sense, perhaps, that Walter Benjamin attributed to the very ambition of history: "To articulate the past historically does not mean to recognize it 'the way it really was.' It means to seize hold of a memory as it flashes up at a moment of danger." This memory is fragile and uncertain enough to awaken our pessimism. Yet if we mention anxiety, here or elsewhere, it is certainly not to paralyze our ability to act but to inject it with an element of doubt, which is the initiating impulse of knowledge. Political thought similarly has value only when it actively challenges contingencies and reversals, spurred by the recognition that the power to act is unbounded.

June 19, 2019

YOUTH

Giovanni Stradano, *Mercato Vecchio, Florence*

Sandro Botticelli, *Spring* (detail)

ONE

THE SEASONS

SPEND THE SUMMER WITH MACHIAVELLI? An odd idea. The author of *The Prince* is hardly an author to take on vacation, a companion for summertime siestas. He is first and foremost a man of action, always doing battle, a man for whom describing the world and giving a clear-eyed account of it is to make progress toward transforming it. "Anyone who reads my work," he said in 1513 about *The Prince*, "will clearly see that in the fifteen years during which I applied myself to the study of government, I was neither nodding off nor wasting time."

His work has been read since his death in 1527 and is still read today, despite his critics and detractors. It invariably rouses us from our torpor. And why not, since Machiavelli is as implacable as the summer sun. It is that celestial orb that gives his words their bite and casts on his subjects such a naked light that the bones show. Nietzsche has said it better than anyone, in *Beyond Good and Evil*: "He lets us breathe the fine, dry air of Florence in his *Prince* and cannot keep from presenting the most serious business in a wild *allegrissimo*, perhaps not without an artist's malicious feeling for the contradiction he is attempting: the thoughts long, heavy, harsh, dangerous, set to a galloping tempo of the finest, most mischievous mood."

But if it's all a matter of rhythm, how could he not have noticed that the *qualita dei tempi*, as he called it, the quality of the times, had reached the autumn of certainty? Italy had been at war since 1494. Proud of its city-states, sure of its cultural preeminence, Italy was nonetheless experiencing unprecedented violence at the hands of the continent's large and predatory monarchical states. This is known as the Italian Wars, a period of great disenchantment. And because the Italian Peninsula had been the laboratory of modern politics for so many centuries, the place where the common future was invented, the approaching war was unmistakably the herald of what would come to be called Europe.

The shadows lengthen, winter steals in, numbing men's souls. Machiavelli knew all this well: the words that freeze behind closed lips, the inability to express what we are becoming. He knew the slow and inexorable slide of a political language into obsolescence. The language he had learned with such delight from books no longer served to accurately render "the actual truth of the matter." When the recent past was no longer any help, why should he not turn toward those he called his "dear Romans," plunge into ancient texts as if into a large, refreshing bath, and give the name "antiquity" to this invigorating way of recasting the future?

Is that what we call the Renaissance? Why not, if we're willing to open our eyes to this spring, whose colors are vapid and innocent only to those who cannot see the brutal ferocity of a Botticelli canvas. Machiavelli is the master of disillusioning. That's why, all through history, he's been a trusted ally in evil times. For my part, I don't think of myself as working on Machiavelli. But with him, yes, as a brother in arms — with the caveat that because he was always a scout, always in the forefront, we must read him not in the present but in the future tense.

All of which is to say something perfectly straightforward: interest in Machiavelli always revives in the course of history when the storm clouds are gathering, because he's the man to philosophize in heavy weather. If we're reading him today, it means we should be worried. He's back: wake up.

Santi di Tito, *Portrait of Niccolò Machiavelli*

TWO

MACHIAVELLIANISM

ORWELLIAN, KAFKAESQUE, SADISTIC. Machiavellian. Having one's name identify a collective anxiety is a dubious honor. In his dictionary of the French language, Émile Littré gives the following definition of "Machiavelli": "Florentine author of the sixteenth century who theorized the practice of violence and tyranny used by the petty tyrants of Italy." A figurative sense is immediately tacked on: "Any statesman lacking principles." Example: "The Machiavellis who rule our fates."

By saddling Machiavelli's name with a figurative meaning, Littré did a strange thing, but history itself did no less. Machiavellianism is what stands between us and Machiavelli. It gives manifest shape to what is evil in politics, it is the hideous face of all that one would like to disavow, but it's hard to close one's eyes to it. It is also a mask behind which the man, Niccolò Machiavelli, who was born in Florence in 1469 and died there in 1527, disappears.

In fact Machiavellianism is not a doctrine Machiavelli formulated, but one that his more malicious adversaries have imputed to him. It's an invention of anti-Machiavellianism. Within fifty years of Machiavelli's death, *The Prince* had taken its place on the Catholic Church's Index of Forbidden Books as a work of the devil, and many political treatises took the title *Anti-Machiavel*. The genre's inventor, a French lawyer and Protestant theologian called Innocent Gentillet, would seem predestined by his name to battle the uglier aspects of the world.

A few years later, it was a brilliant Jesuit, an ardent Counter-Reformationist, who took up the cudgels against Machiavelli. His name was Giovanni Botero, and he invented the concept of "reason of state," a concept immediately ascribed to Machiavelli, since it suggests that the state knows no law or requirement other than self-preservation.

From that point on, Machiavellianism ran like an underground river below the foundations of European political theory, silently eating away at them and occasionally resurfacing into view. Machiavelli persists, wearing a mask: we recognize him behind one or another of his borrowed names; we deduce his ideas from those that are given supposedly in opposition.

Gustave Flaubert, writing around the same time as Émile Littré, produced a *Dictionary of Conventional Wisdom* that defines both "Machiavellianism" and "Machiavelli" — in that order — with the first providing a screen for the second. "Machiavellianism. A word never pronounced without a shudder." Then: "Machiavelli. One hasn't read him but thinks him a scoundrel."

It's all in how you look at him, then. And why not take a look at him for ourselves, fearlessly; why not lift the mask to see the monster? We need only read his works to actually meet him, this man who was so intensely a part of his own time, and who for that reason continually invites himself into ours. Nothing is easier, in fact, because Machiavelli doesn't bother to hide, unless it's behind the banality of his own existence. But when he talks about himself, he does so frankly and in no way underplays his loneliness, his joy, or his doubts. Here, for instance, are a few lines into which he pours his troubles:

I hope and hope increases my torment,
I weep and weeping feeds my bruised heart,
I laugh and my laughter does not touch my soul,
I burn and no one sees my passion
I fear what I see and what I hear,
All things bring me renewed pain.
Thus hoping, I weep and laugh and burn,
And I fear what I hear and see.

Peter Paul Rubens, *Portrait of Lorenzo de' Medici*

THREE

1469, TIME RETURNS

NICCOLÒ MACHIAVELLI WAS BORN on May 3, 1469, in Florence. But what was Florence in 1469? A republic of swaggering princes. A republic, yes, but swollen with pride, vaunting its power and prosperity, ornamenting with brilliant Latin its long record as a commune, which had made the city a model of self-government for almost three centuries. A republic, but one governed by men of wealth, and gradually settling into oligarchy.

Among the powerful were the Medici, rich bankers who had dominated the government for the past thirty years. The first to gain prominence was Cosimo. He conducted his affairs discreetly, out of the view of his supporters and clients. Avoiding the pomp of a royal court, he lived soberly, with the gravity befitting a powerful man who wanted to be seen as the father of his country. His son Piero succeeded him in 1464, and he gradually shed the restraints of republicanism. Five years on, in 1469, it was known throughout Florence that Piero was ill. He would die on December 2. Then came the grandson, Lorenzo. He was twenty years old, and the future of the House of

Medici was in his hands. Before long, he would be known as the Magnificent, because of his reckless spending. He impetuously took the lead in every procession, displaying the hundreds of pearls and precious stones that studded his velvet cap. Dressed as a prince, he exposed himself to public view — that is, as Machiavelli would later understand, he made a spectacle of himself and courted danger.

Danger, what danger? In order to entertain the gilded youth of the Tuscan city, a tournament was organized on February 7, 1469. All that remained of the warlike games that had once punctuated the political life of the Italian communes was a refined simulacrum, a sumptuous parade, as showy as a dance step. No violence was on offer, unless it was the spectacle of domination itself. Under the jealous gaze of the onlookers, Lorenzo flourished his impressive banner, emblazoned with his motto in gold letters, written in French, the language of the knightly romances that Europe's gentry still mooned over. It read: *Le temps revient*, "Time returns."

So that is the Renaissance, then: a renewal, the refreshed vigor of an eternal spring, Italy rediscovering its golden age by ripping aside a heavy curtain of darkness. It took the youthful energy of this young prince to greet the newly returned time. Not the past, but that active, live, and creative part of the past the humanists called *antiquitas*, in contrast to what is worn, old, and beyond use. But as the new and shining day is trumpeted, have we any assurance that it will be anything but the parodic reenactment of an imagined past?

We are familiar with Guy Debord's prophetic 1967 work *The Society of the Spectacle*. We have therefore been warned about the pernicious effects of commodity fetishism and the frenzied acclamation it generates. But alas, prophets never give advance warning of the great catastrophes. Those that were brewing in Florence in 1469 went undetected. Machiavelli was born on May 3, three months after Lorenzo's triumph, and he soon had the sense that he'd been born too late. What he was left with was lucidity, the weapon of the despairing.

Giuseppe Alinari, *Ponte Vecchio, Florence*

FOUR

A FATHER'S AMBITION

LET'S ACKNOWLEDGE that he often exaggerates. When he writes "I was born poor and learned to work before having fun," frankly, he's exaggerating. True, Machiavelli was never a member of that carefree youthful generation "whose only care," he would later write in his *History of Florence*, "was to appear splendid in their dress, wise and cunning in their witticisms." Because to be a member of that set, in the time of Lorenzo the Magnificent, you had to belong to one of the venerable aristocratic families with vast rural landholdings, the *magnati*.

The Machiavelli family lived below the level of those magnates. But they were not exactly poor. They subsisted, though frugally, from the rent of their land, as they had done for several centuries already. Their straitened circumstances were the result of bad political choices. One of the family's forebears, Girolamo Machiavelli, had tried to stir opposition to the Medici and was arrested, banished, tortured, and thrown into prison, where he died in 1460. This was the flip side of the great feast of the Medici.

Niccolò, born nine years later, in 1469, had only two older sisters, but the family house in the Oltrarno district, on the far side of Florence's river, was chock-full of people all the same. Cousins and brothers-in-law crowded in, a whole happy, noisy *brigata*, in the normal way of extended families — a model Niccolò Machiavelli would re-create once he was married. The house, which looked onto the Ponte Vecchio, was destroyed in 1944. A few years later, historians found a book that documented its history. It was the family record kept by Messer Bernardo Machiavelli, father of Niccolò. He was addressed as "Messer" because he was a doctor of law, but the family's anti-Medician taint probably kept him from pursuing a legal career.

Coldly, methodically, Bernardo recorded the minute facts of family life. There are no private outpourings in the *Libro di Ricordi*, which is less a journal than a meticulous accounting of household affairs. It reminds us that all power starts at home, with the management of things and persons, of resources and emotions, and most especially with a close attention to detail.

Bernardo patiently took note of everything that came into the house: wine, nuts, wives, and books. Many books, more and more books. Law, history, literature. What if the solution lay there? The powerful used legitimate culture as a weapon. What we call humanism describes above all the art of drawing distinctions, which the Florentine elite practiced with an arrogance we have difficulty imagining today. In any case, culture lay beyond the Machiavellis' reach. Niccolò would not have an illustrious tutor, nor go to university, nor learn Greek. He was therefore not a humanist, and those who prided themselves on that distinction held it over him all his life.

But Florence was full of little schools where Latin was taught, and Gutenberg's invention, only a few years old when Bernardo took up his pen, was becoming more and more widespread. Bernardo inventoried thirty books, some of which he bought at a very steep price. In order to afford Livy's *History of Rome*, he contracted with the publisher to draw up an index of its "towns, mountains, and rivers," a task that cost him nine months of work. This, too, was something Machiavelli inherited: his father's ambition. That ambition was focused on books, on the hope that they might offer revenge, on the certainty that an opponent's closely held weapons could be turned against him.

Giuseppe Alinari, *View of Florence from Monte alle Croci*

TITI
LVCRETII CARI
DE RERVM NATVRA
LIBRI SEX.

A DIONYSIO LAMBINO
Monstroliensi litterarum Græcarum in vrbe Lutetia
doctore Regio, locis innumerabilibus ex auctori-
tate quinque codicum manu scriptorum
emendati, atque in antiquum ac
natiuum statum ferè restituti,
& præterea breuibus, &
perquàm vtilibus
commentariis
illustrati.

PARISIIS,
Et Lugduni habentur.

In Gulielmi Rouillij,
Et Philippi G. Rouillij Nep.
ædibus, via Iacobæa sub Concordia.

CVM PRIVILEGIO REGIS.

TEM KE
PO SVR
RVM REC
&RI TIO.
RVM 1563.

Title page from Lucretius, *On the Nature of Things*

FIVE

STORY OF A DANGEROUS BOOK

THERE ARE BOOKS YOU HANG ON TO as though they were life buoys. When everything around you is pitching, when capsize seems inevitable, they stay afloat, they emit a signal, they save you from shipwreck. Machiavelli's books are of that kind. Throughout history, they have been the faithful allies of those who sought to understand the drift of politics.

You can read in order to find out where you are, but you can also read in order to get lost. An ancient text, coming from afar, can start to command attention, make wild claims, knock everything around it out of kilter. And suddenly it's altering the course of our lives. In the first century BCE, the Latin poet Lucretius had a word for this deviation. He called it *"clinamen."* In his *De rerum natura*, or *On the Nature of Things*, Lucretius voices the song of the world — a world that has no creator, where nature constantly reinvents itself. Because everything is made of atoms, our souls as well as all things, attracted by their own weight.

But here's the thing: if all the particles fell through the void in straight lines, nothing would exist except for an endless day of rain. Here I quote Lucretius: "At uncertain intervals, the atoms swerve slightly out of their course — just enough to say that there has been an alteration in their movement." At that point, freedom is possible, time is possible, the world is possible. It's clear why Lucretius's materialist poetry, in which Greek epicurean philosophy is set to Roman music, was considered a handbook of atheism in modern times. A dangerous book, a book that swerves, that derails the world and knocks it off its hinges.

So, Machiavelli read this book. He not only read it but also recopied it. Laboriously, he transcribed the Latin poem. Because books were rare at the time, those who loved them paid a hefty price for them, putting in the time to write them out, with aching backs and bleary eyes. Remember how Niccolò's father, Bernardo Machiavelli, bought a copy of Livy by providing the book with an index. Niccolò, by copying Lucretius, was doing the same thing. The task completed, he scrawled his name on the manuscript, which is preserved today in the Vatican library, where his signature allowed scholars to identify it.

Is that what it is to be a historian? To read over the shoulder of another person reading? The year is possibly 1497; Machiavelli is not yet thirty. In his hands, he holds the book that will probably make his life swerve. For what is his philosophy, in the end, if not the translation into politics of Lucretius's materialism? Things can be counted on, says the poet, always to produce an image that will obscure their true nature. To govern, or to learn how not to let oneself be governed (which is to say, to understand political realities), requires ripping aside the veil of appearances. Because they, the realities, are what will be acting behind that veil.

To no longer be ruled by these realities, one has to abandon any belief in the existence of a golden age. The idea, however, was one that the Florentine elite of the quattrocento found particularly heady. They called it by the flattering name of "Neoplatonism" and decorated it with fluttering draperies, as in a Botticelli image. This is the game that Lucretius comes along and disrupts. For in the fifth book of *On the Nature of Things*, he describes the original violence of primitive man. From it we inherited a fear of man's origins, of the time when we wandered "like wild beasts" and, as Lucretius writes, led a vagabond life. Machiavelli would remember this passage when the first accounts of the New World reached him. He would also remember it when he undertook to describe the new world of a politics based on the art of managing our dissensions without too much violence, on coming to an agreement over our disagreements.

Was Lucretius's *De rerum natura* a dangerous book? Less than has been suggested. Some historians have advanced the notion that its rediscovery in 1417 by the humanist Poggio Bracciolini made the world swerve from its course, pushed it toward the modern age. The concept is tempting: it enlarges the role of literature in human society, which is agreeable to men of letters. But it assigns too much power to the written word. Books never produce revolutions. They become our allies only when we are ready to read them. They are masters of freedom, true, but only for those who are sufficiently free already.

"I walk along ways no man has trodden," writes Lucretius. And Machiavelli took after him in his *Discourses on the First Ten Books of Titus Livius*:

> I have decided to set out on an untrodden path, aware that this will bring me trouble and hardship.

What trouble and hardship? We will soon see.

Joseph Vigier, *Path of Chaos* (detail)

A TIME FOR ACTION

Jean Bourdichon, *Louis XII Leaves the City of Alessandria*

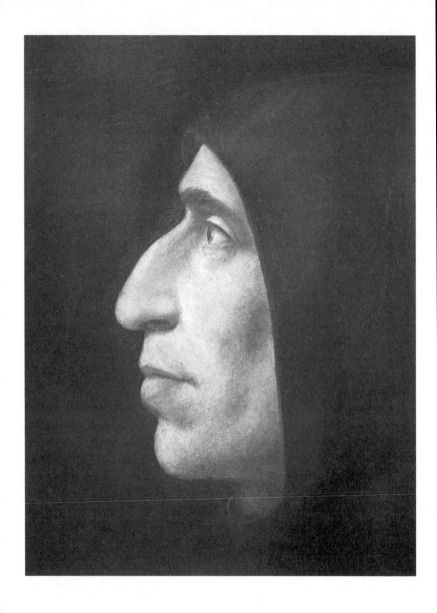

Fra Bartolomeo, *Portrait of Savonarola*

SUDDENLY SAVONAROLA

HE LISTENS. Fascinated, terrified, perhaps admiring. On this day in 1498, in Florence, Machiavelli is listening to Savonarola. He listens as the friar bends the crowd under the weight of his words. How is it that people allow themselves to be subjugated by the force of words — "bewitched," as he would later write? And this fiery Dominican friar who claims inspiration from God, does he really believe in what he is prophesying? "As I surmise," wrote Machiavelli, "the friar is adapting to the times and shifting his lies accordingly." This is the first public letter of Machiavelli's still in our possession, written as the events of 1498 reached a pitch of intensity, and already there was talk of the political art of dissimulation.

Savonarola had been governing Florence for four years. Or rather, he led but not in his own name. He called down upon the city the shadow of a vengeful God. For his decrees were formulated in heaven, and from thence they came. The Church must be scourged, he fulminated, and society reformed — which is to say converted. And what justified and compelled this reform was a keen awareness of guilt.

What was going on? The town was thronged with penitents, the "weepers," whom Savonarola's enemies, the "hotheads," were violently assaulting in the streets. No one was allowed to take the middle ground. Children were made to denounce their parents if they fell short of being good Christians. Savonarola led the charge against those who were hypocrites — a favorite target of every brand of fanaticism. He ordered the bonfires of the vanities, on which women's luxury items and overly refined church ornaments were burned. It was even said that Sandro Botticelli, who painted *The Birth of Venus*, was convinced to sacrifice a number of his canvases.

What was happening? Why, it was politics, as always. Born in Ferrara to a family of physicians, Girolamo Savonarola followed a brilliant course in humanistic studies, which he converted into a sustained hatred for the world. In Italy at that time, there was a coterie of apocalyptic prophets who traveled from town to town displaying their skill at painting the future in dark terms. By bringing him to Florence, Lorenzo the Magnificent thought he could put him to use. But Lorenzo died in 1492, and there followed a time of uncertainty and fear.

Savonarola fanned this fear from the Monastery of San Marco and gave it a focus: the coming war. This war, he said, would have the face of an enemy from abroad. And lo, the prophecy came to pass: in 1494, a king from over the mountains, Charles VIII of France, crossed the

Alps and began to overrun the Italian city-states. The Medici fled as the conquerors advanced, leaving a glaring political void. It was they, the Medici, who had dug the dark hole in the very heart of the republican institutions of the Florentine commune, hollowing it out from the inside and never acknowledging what had sapped the city of its vitality: their authoritarian power.

We now often speak of theocracy to describe the moment when religion steps into the breach, fills the void, and takes the place of politics. But politics is never abolished entirely. Prophets describe the future to have an effect on the present. On May 22, 1498, at sunset, Savonarola would tell his judges, "The things that happen quickly in God's eyes may take longer on earth." Not always; they can also be accelerated. The next day he would be dead.

Woodcut from Savonarola, *Sermon on the Art of Dying Well*

Florentine painter after Francesco Rosselli, *The Execution of Savonarola*

SEVEN

A YOUNG MAN IN POLITICS

IF YOU VISIT the Piazza della Signoria in Florence, you'll see the commemorative plaque. It marks the place where Savonarola was tortured. There, at the heart of the civic space, in the midst of a great crowd, the friar who had held the town under the sway of his prophetic speech for four years was hanged and burned. Children, perhaps the very same who, a few weeks before, had lit the bonfires of the vanities for him, scattered his ashes in the Arno. It was May 23, 1498. The wheel of Fortune, that blind goddess who takes pleasure in bringing down the proud, had pivoted on its axis.

The plots, intrigues, and changes in alliance that brought about Savonarola's downfall are unimportant. The one thing that Machiavelli retained was that when Pope Alexander VI finally brought together his disparate coalition in a united front against Savonarola, the friar walked away from the fight. Worse, by clinging to the pacific ideals of a Christian republic, he invited the violence of those who still resented being powerless. As Machiavelli would later write in *The Prince*, in a phrase as finely turned as a reversal of fortune, Savonarola was an unarmed prophet. The task at hand was to take up his political plan at the point where he left off, resolving the matters left in suspense: the question of a leader, the question of force, the question of the state of emergency.

In point of fact, the time had come; the opportunity was at hand. By making the Great Council the primary organ of Florentine government, Savonarola had restored the republic. Machiavelli was not a member of that government, but places were opening up, the political purge had begun. Who would replace Savonarola's allies in the chancery? Machiavelli was twenty-nine years old, he had no political experience, and he was untainted by any association with the fallen government. His father was a close friend of Florence's first chancellor, the celebrated humanist Bartolomeo Scala. Niccolò Machiavelli had neither the birth, nor the education, nor the connections to aspire to such high office, but first secretary of the second chancery, why not? It was less well paid and less prestigious but, as we would say today, more strategic — a discreet and influential position of responsibility.

His duties were to maintain a daily correspondence with the allies of the Florentine state and to monitor the stew of opinions that was stirring up the common people. Bartolomeo Scala often said to Machiavelli's father: "It was the people's sewer." Descending into the lower depths of human passions, not wrinkling one's nose at the stench of political power, which Machiavelli would refer to as the "art of government" — this was his calling.

On June 19, 1498, three weeks after Savonarola's execution, the Great Council confirmed Machiavelli to his new office. He gathered a small team of men around him who would follow him until 1512. None was yet thirty years old. They were lawyers and men of letters. Above all, they were hungry — for work, for power, and for friendships. For fifteen years, this happy crew shared everything, indecent jokes and secrets of state, heedless of the conventions established by the clergy, who had for so long kept Florentine civil society static.

A government is also defined by the age of those in key posts: behind the juvenile pomp of the court of the Medici, a gerontocracy had held the reins of power. Exhausted, they had let go their hold. It was the moment to grab the reins. Machiavelli would later make it his maxim: "Try your luck, for Fortune is a friend of the young, and be willing to adjust with the times." The time had come; things could finally start.

Still from *Zero for Conduct*

Workshop of Jean Perréal, *Portrait of King Louis XII*

EIGHT

TRAVEL

"GO FORTH OUT OF YOUR HOMES and take stock of those around you." This from a letter dated 1503. Machiavelli was addressing the *Dieci di libertà*, the ten magistrates who directed the Republic of Florence's military operations in keeping with their idea of freedom. Was it an encouragement to travel? Let's call it instead a forceful exhortation to upend settled convictions. Travel, venture out of your familiar surroundings, quit your sitting posture, abandon the comfortable peace of your deeprooted home. From elsewhere, you'll see other things, but above all you'll see the place from which you normally view the world. Is this not what the painters of the Renaissance called perspective?

> Go forth out of your homes and take stock of those around you. You will find yourself surrounded by two or three towns that are more interested in your death than in your life. Continue on beyond the borders of Tuscany and consider all of Italy: you will find that it is subjugated to the king of France, the Venetians, the pope, and the duke of Valentinois.

Florence from the viewpoint of Tuscany, Tuscany from the viewpoint of Italy, Italy from the viewpoint of Europe, and — why not? — Europe from the viewpoint of the expanding world. Machiavelli worked at the chancery with Agostino Vespucci, whose cousin, Amerigo, a naval explorer and geographer, would give his name — his first name anyway — to the New World. You grasp the idea: what Machiavelli wanted to gain by urging the magistrates to go beyond their familiar perspective was above all a map of the relations between the powers.

Machiavelli did not have the rank of ambassador. On his diplomatic missions, he did not represent the government of Florence or have the authority to negotiate. But he could observe, discuss, and compare. In Romagna, under Cesare Borgia, who was Pope Alexander VI's son (and also the Duke of Valentinois), he learned about the speed needed in making decisions, the art of surprising the world around him, and the ruthlessness required of a ruler in conducting politics. In Rome, to which he traveled twice, he became aware of the outsized power of the pope and realized how quickly all of Italy would be destabilized if the pope acted as a warrior prince in the temporal world without abandoning his spiritual claims to universal power. The court of Maximilian I, the Holy Roman Emperor, inspired his reflections on sovereignty in his *Portrait of the Affairs of Germany*. But France was where he would encounter true power.

Four times, Machiavelli traveled to the court of Louis XII: in 1500, 1504, 1510, and 1511. It is hard for us today to grasp how extraordinarily powerful France's great monarchy was. The territory of France was "fat and opulent," its system of taxation highly effective, and its long-established custom of submission to authority untroubled by any tradition of freedom: this is what struck Machiavelli. And, most astonishingly, the French seemed to like their king.

The Florentine envoy was badly treated at Louis XII's court, particularly during his first mission in 1500. He met with evasiveness and contempt, and his views were ignored by all. Initially, he was indignant: the ministers were "blinded by their own power." But then he understood: the king of France "esteemed no one unless that person was armed or had something to give." Therefore, good sirs, wrote Machiavelli to his masters in Florence, "you are valued as nothing" — and he used the Latin words to drive the nail home: *pro nihilo*.

To the arrogant French who reproached him "with understanding nothing about war," Machiavelli would reply later in *The Prince* that they "understood nothing about government." But for the moment, he swallowed the reproach — and took his humiliation as a lesson in politics. Travel is an exercise in disorientation. It also gives a healthy boost to your sense of modesty.

N.a. 1223

✝

Rapporto di Cose della magna p. Nicolò Machia
a gli Sig.ri q̃ governo di 17. di Giugno 1508:

L'Imperatore del mese di Giugno passato l'adrieto ad Costanza
di tutti i principi della magna p. far provisione alla sua pas-
sata in Italia alla Corona, farsele il suo moto p. proprio, e per
essere ancora sollicitato del breue del pontefice et gli prometteur
grandi aiuti per passar d'Italia: Chiese l'Imperatore alla Dieta
p. 7 mesi prossimi iij^m Cavalli et xx^m fanti et promise di andar in
persona di suo proprio infino in Roma persona: la cagione p. che eba
dandosi si poco senza tanta impresa finta p̃ e credessi
che passino guadagnandosi potersi valere de venizani et d'altri di
Italia con appresso feliran Ne credessi mai ct li venizani gli im-
trassino hauendoli questi poco innanzi gran esercito di francia, dopo
l'acquisto di Genova: p.a hauevan alloro richiesta mandato circa
a due milia persona a Vrouso, hauevan messo voce di volere ragunar
i principi, et stavono insuperiti aminacciare e fuisser sendo si pri
trovan da Pisa: Ilust. Fore, et il re luigi subito preso Genova
sono ritorno a lione dicendo et parendo allo Imperatore hauer loro

NINE

THE CUTTING EDGE OF LANGUAGE

TRAVELING AND WRITING. That is how Machiavelli "studied the art of government." Going somewhere and seeing for himself, and, if he couldn't do that, exchanging a volley of letters, those tireless travelers, with his far-flung correspondents. From 1498 to 1512, for fifteen years, Florence's secretary of the chancery composed thousands of dispatches, reports, and diplomatic letters destined for every part of Europe. The flood of these letters formed a rhythmic swell, accelerated at times by the backwash of the political *tempo*. Then he would take up his pen several times a day, or dictate in haste, to recount a development, obtain information, fire off questions, or test someone's will. At times, the urge was too strong. Swept up by the pull of a detail, the momentum of his story, he would race off down the page, formulating the incisive turns of phrase that make up the glorious nastiness of his style.

Because that was the game: to sharpen in the fire of action the stylus of political language, and to keep its edge from growing dull in case one needed to slice into the raw. Historians have said that fifteenth-century Italy invented diplomacy. Developed on the scale of the Italian Peninsula between small city-states that needed to maintain their power balance, the new techniques would extend in the following century to all of Europe, which thus became, in the game of war and peace, a large-scale Italy.

Machiavelli, whose career spanned the old century and the new, witnessed this change. He inherited a tradition, which he revived and reinvigorated — the tradition of embassies, but also of the common language of negotiation, which at the time was Italian. Let's not go imagining that Machiavelli created this way of speaking. It was also his job to draw up the minutes of informal gatherings of influential citizens, when they were being consulted on important matters — and thousands of such pages have come down to us. He thus put himself in tune with a social discourse whose rhythms he constantly heard, and it was by giving musical voice to his own pulsations that he elaborated something like a political language.

I'd like to have you hear the joy and swiftness of this speech, which runs straight toward what Machiavelli calls the *verità effetuale della cosa*, the actual truth of the thing. It is discernible from the start, unmistakably, in his first public address. In May 1499, he spoke about matters relating to Pisa, Florence's eternal rival. What was to be done? Listen:

> As no one doubts that Florence must regain Pisa if it wants to maintain its independence, I do not feel I need to argue the matter with other reasons than those we already know. I will examine only the ways that can

or will lead to our regaining Pisa, which are either by force or by love. In other words, either we will besiege Pisa, or Pisa will willingly throw herself into our arms.

Machiavelli goes on to say that love is preferable, but that force is sometimes inevitable.

"As force is necessary, I believe we must now weigh whether it behooves us to use it in such times as these."

Did he say "now"? Then a decision needs to be made:

"We must obtain Pisa either by siege and famine, or by an assault from our artillery drawn up under its walls."

And it continues in this vein — either this or that — by following the successive branching of possibilities. Are you catching the rhythm? It is the Machiavellian *tempo*, which gives his speech its sure and rapid pace. To make a decision, you need to resolve a question once and for all. But you cannot settle anything without knowing the alternatives.

Giuseppe Alinari, *Veduta Generale, Pisa*

Ridolfo del Ghirlandaio, *Portrait of Piero Soderini*

TEN

COUP D'ETAT

MACHIAVELLI HAD THE GOOD FORTUNE always to be disappointed by the statesmen he met. None, it turned out, measured up to the situation; none was ready to act with the sharpness, decisiveness, and speed that the quality of the times demanded. It was good fortune, in a way, when you consider the moral and literary depths to which intellectuals can descend when they become entranced with a powerful figure. If that figure captures their admiration, their intelligence soon capitulates.

Machiavelli tried to find princes to admire, but when he found none he was forced to invent a *Prince* on paper. And that one is still talked about today: the fiction has become more substantial than the fleeting ghosts of the powerful also-rans of history. Who today remembers Piero Soderini? He was the gonfalonier, the chief elected officer of the Florentine state, who made Machiavelli his protégé. A "patient and kindly" man, Machiavelli would later write, but political patience is the opposite of irresolution or slowness: it has less to do with taking one's time than with seizing opportunity when it is offered.

Soderini did not see the danger threatening Florence, nor did he think to arm himself against his enemies, and, in 1512, Machiavelli held him responsible for the fall of the government he had so ardently defended. When Soderini died ten years later, in 1522, Machiavelli wrote a cruel epigram about him. The soul of the deposed gonfalonier stands at the gates of hell:

"You'd enter hell?" says Hades. "Poor feckless bimbo,
With all the other children, you'll spend eternity in limbo."

Curtain. The fallen get no pity. And Machiavelli showed no pity when he described Cesare Borgia's exit from the stage in 1503. For a time, he had been interested in Borgia's little theater of cruelty, but history had moved its arena elsewhere than Florence or Romagna. A major spectacle was about to be mounted in Italy, the confrontation of the great European monarchies: the Holy Roman Empire, the kingdom of France, and Spain, which Pope Julius II would reinsert into the game in 1511.

Then things happened very fast. On April 11, 1512, the king of France was victorious in Ravenna, but at such great cost that he was obliged to withdraw from Italy. With his allies, he decided to put the Medici back in power in Florence. On September 16, the Medici partisans seized the Palazzo della Signoria and dissolved the Great Council, the central organ of the Florentine Republic. This coup d'état prompted a disorganized conspiracy among freedom-loving youths of good family.

Either from clumsiness or design, a list of their accomplices was circulated, and Machiavelli's name was on it.

It was over. He lost his post, went to prison, and suffered torture on several occasions. He was on the point of being executed, and what saved his skin was the strange atmosphere of patriotic fervor and reconciliation that followed the election, on March 11, 1513, of the young cardinal Giovanni de' Medici to the papacy as Pope Leo X. Now Machiavelli was in exile, the victim of what he called a "malignancy of fortune." Was it the influence of the dark star known by the Italians as *disastro*? This was no time to lift his eyes to heaven like a terrified child. He had to act to avert disaster, find a way to climb back into the political ring. But how? Would books, once again, help him get revenge?

Palazzo della Signoria, Florence

AFTER
DISASTER

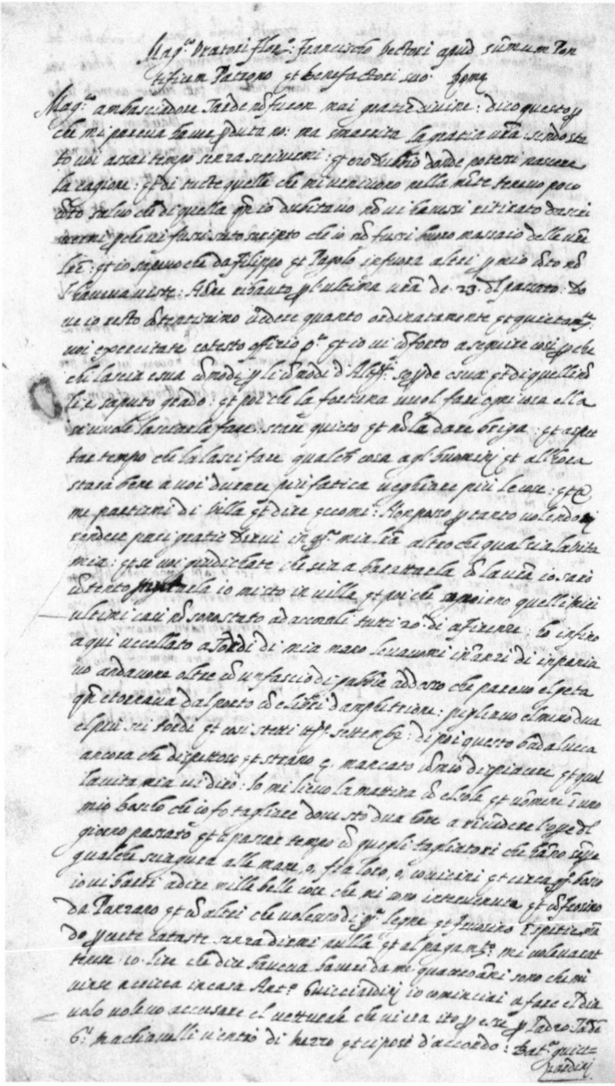

Letter from Machiavelli to Francesco Vettori

ELEVEN

AN EXILE'S LETTER

"I AM ON MY FARM, and since my recent problems I have not been twenty days in Florence." It is December 10, 1513, and Machiavelli is writing his friend Francesco Vettori. This letter is the journal of his crushing defeat. Driven from Florence by the return of the Medici, whose arrival quells all hope of a republic, Machiavelli is a beaten man. And so he writes, incessantly. Not to ward off the blows — it's too late for that — but to understand in hindsight why he didn't see them coming.

> I shall tell you what my life is. I rise in the morning with the sun and head over to some woods I am having cut down, where I stay two hours surveying the work that was done the day before and to spend some time with the woodcutters, who are always in the middle of some dispute, either among themselves or with their neighbors. And I could tell you a thousand amusing things about these woods that have happened to me.

A thousand amusing things, yes, because enlivened by his literary reminiscing. He looks at the countryside, and it calls Petrarch to mind. Now he is wandering off, a book of poetry under his arm:

> Leaving the woods, I go to a spring, and from there to one of my bird traps. I have a book under my arm, either Dante or Petrarch.

Look, now he is coming back:

> Then I walk down the road to the tavern, speak to pass-ersby, ask them news of their villages.

Machiavelli is a hunter, always on the lookout for the mechanism that moves human passions and acts on the lives of others. Where is politics to be grasped if not among ordinary people, when differences of opinion arise? At the tavern are "a butcher, a miller, and two kiln tenders. With these men I dawdle all day playing cards and backgammon, which results in a thousand quarrels with streams of spiteful and wounding words."

At nightfall, finally, it is time for Machiavelli to pay a visit to his invisible friends who live in ancient books. They died a long time ago, but they sustain us. They, too, can be asked for news. But for that, you need to go to a little trouble, make yourself presentable, to join sol-emnly in conversation with the men of antiquity:

> When evening comes, I return home and go into my study. At the door I take off my everyday clothes, cov-ered with mud and dirt, and don garments of court and palace. Now garbed fittingly I step into the ancient

courts of men of antiquity, where, received kindly, I partake of food that is for me alone and for which I was born, where I am not ashamed to converse with them and ask them the reasons for their actions. And they in their full humanity answer me. For four hours I feel no tedium and forget every anguish, not afraid of poverty, not terrified by death.

I am unaware of any finer panegyric to the transmission of ideas from one age to another — this joyous and respectful way of cutting through the crowd without overly cherishing one's own company, of enlarging the circle of common humanity to include the living and the dead. So spoke Machiavelli in 1513, in a letter addressed to a friend, to tell him how he avoided "the mold overcoming his brain" since he had been pushed out of politics. Oh! I was forgetting. He also told his friend he had just finished a little book. Its title you already know: *The Prince*.

2. G.B.Q.   8287.

NICCOLO MACHIA
VELLI ALMAGH
IFICO LOREZO
DE MEDICI

ogliono el piu delle uolte co
loro ch desiderano acquistar
gratia appsso auno principe forsch
incotro con qlle cose ch infra le loro
habbino piu chare o delle ghi ueghi
lui delectarsi: d onde si uede molte
uolte es loro presentato caualli,
armi drappi doro pietre pretiose
et simili ornamenti degni della gra
dezza di quelli. Desiderando io adunq
offrirmi alla .m. v. con qlch testi
moni della seruitu mia uerso di
quella non ho trouato intra la mia

Dedication page from Machiavelli, *The Prince*

TWELVE

HOW TO READ *THE PRINCE*

AND WHAT IF HE WAS JUST A BASTARD? In the figurative sense that Jean-Paul Sartre gave the word, of course, as I wouldn't otherwise presume: a bastard, unlike a heel, believes that his existence is indispensable to the functioning of the world. Machiavelli doesn't just write *The Prince* to make up for being out of the game or to take revenge on his enemies. He is chomping at the bit to return to politics and chafing at being unable to make use of his knowledge of statecraft, gathered, as he writes in the book's dedication, "through [his] long experience of modern affairs and a lifelong study of ancient times."

Would he do anything to win the favor of those currently in power? One might well think so from reading the surprising dedication: "Niccolò Machiavelli to His Magnificence Lorenzo de' Medici." This refers to Lorenzo the Younger, on whom Pope Leo X conferred the government of Florence in the summer of 1513. How can Machiavelli curry favor with a member of the Medici family, which brought about his downfall and destroyed

Florence's republican government? Is he being untrue to his own principles, or is he playing a double game?

Treachery, duplicity: it's hard for us to suspend our judgment of this book, although its whole program is to uncouple political action from conventional morality. The truth is that we don't really know how to read *The Prince*. This is not a new development: arguments over Machiavellianism have always centered on the question not so much of why but for whom Machiavelli wrote. For princes, or for those wanting to resist them? In the eighteenth century, Diderot held that it was for the former: Machiavelli is giving instruction to the powerful, teaching them "a detestable sort of politics that can be captured in three words, the art of tyranny." But Jean-Jacques Rousseau, in *The Social Contract*, took the other side: "This man has nothing to teach tyrants, they already know perfectly well what they must do. He is instructing the people on what they have to fear."

Is Machiavelli good, then, or is he evil? However much we would like to have an answer to this question, it's better to set it aside. For if we want to know whom Machiavelli is addressing in *The Prince*, we need only turn to Chapter 15, where he says: "My intention is to write something useful for discerning minds." This is a revolutionary gesture par excellence: to describe accurately how things happen, and to leave the task of drawing up the ensuing rules of action to others.

I intentionally call him "revolutionary," as you'll understand from seeing the context of his statement. The passage deals with the domination that princes exert over their subjects.

> Many have written about this, and I fear I might be considered presumptuous, particularly as I intend to depart from the principles laid down by others. As my intention is to write something useful for discerning minds, I find it more fitting to seek the truth of the matter rather than imaginary conceptions. Many have imagined republics and principalities that have never been seen or heard of.

When he departs from "the principles laid down by others," he abandons all of political philosophy. The time is past for imagining better forms of government. Let's start by laying down exactly how power is handled, by taking stock of it implacably. And afterward? Afterward, we can always see. At least we will have been warned.

PENGUIN CLASSICS

NICCOLÒ MACHIAVELLI

The Prince

A new translation by TIM PARKS

Machiavelli, *The Prince*

THIRTEEN

TO CONQUER AND PRESERVE

THE BOOK OF MACHIAVELLI'S commonly known as *The Prince* is actually called *De principatibus*, or "Of Principalities." What difference does that make, and why was posterity so quick to forget it? Machiavelli, as we now realize, was not writing a treatise of good government. He was not lecturing anyone, neither those in government nor those who read him. In that, at least, he was breaking the mirror, by which I mean the "mirror for princes," a traditional medieval literary genre that offered moral instruction to crowned heads by presenting variations on the theme that to govern was the opposite of to dominate.

Machiavelli, that master of disillusion, has the following to say: let us stop taking our wishes for realities and stop dreaming of imaginary republics conjured by fine words, and let us start instead to take an inventory of the different methods of governing according to our experience. *De principatibus*: the book announces itself as a typology, even if Machiavelli's scathing style is constantly running away with his sensibly ordered project, suddenly veering from the plan he has announced and thrusting ahead by quick jabs and overlapping sequences of digressions — as though the headstrong text were generating itself along the way.

One distinction is posited from the outset, however, which Machiavelli holds to. He is not discussing republics but principalities, and not principalities one inherits but those that one has conquered, by force, by guile, or by luck: those principalities, in effect, that come under the sway of bold heroes of fortune, new princes. Now, let us not deceive ourselves; it is much easier to seize power than to hold on to it. In Machiavelli's language, *mantenere lo stato* means both to preserve the state and to maintain one's own position. Those who prove unable to do so not only ruin their chance of prevailing over the long term — which remains the great aim of politics — but also diminish the state in its sovereignty, its government, and its institutional strength.

After one has boldly seized power, it takes special qualities to maintain one's grip on it, and those qualities are different from the ones touted in common morality. Starting in the fifteenth chapter, there is a change of plan, a reversal of perspective: Machiavelli explores the virtues that make a prince the unscrupulous virtuoso of his own self-preservation. His treatise takes on another dimension, brilliant and provocative. This explains why, when it was first published, posthumously, in 1532, his Roman editor, Antonio Blado, gave it a more catchy title, in Italian: *Il principe*, the prince.

This is the title, of course, that posterity would retain. It invites a reading that both simplifies and generalizes the work, reducing it to a handbook on decision-making, a treatise on the right moment to act, useful to all professionals occupied with the government of persons and things, those (to use an ugly word) in management. At that point, "the prince" becomes a generic term, depending on the context, for the government, the political party, the chief officer, or the multitude. It speaks to the urgency of reading Machiavelli in the present moment.

τὰ πάλιν ὅτι μὲ εἴζιν ἐκέλθοιν.
ἢ ἀῇς μίαν μὲ ἴδω πάντων σωρά-
σαδ, ἐ αὐτῆ βραχύτι καλέλασαν· ἢ
ὀμέων πρὸς αὐτὰν, τίσσε ὦ βελτί-
ςα Διαιρεῖν οὕτως ἐδίδαξεν· ἢ δ᾽-
Εἶπεν, ἡ τοῦ ὄνου σύμφορά· ἰῶτμεν·
Ὁ μῦθος δηλοῖ, ὅτι σωφρονίζεοι τῖ-
μονται τοῖς ἀνθρώποις τὰ τῶν πέ-
λας διςτυήματα :•

Gherardo del Fora, *The Lion, the Bear, and the Fox*

FOURTEEN

EVIL IN POLITICS

IN CHAPTER 18 of *The Prince*, there is a story of the kind we tell to frighten children. It could be called "The Fox and the Lion." Those who rule over us, says Machiavelli, know how to act like animals, sometimes cunning, sometimes strong and forceful. Depending on the circumstances, they choose to act like the fox or the lion, "for the lion cannot defend himself against traps, and the fox cannot defend himself against wolves. Therefore, one must be a fox to recognize traps, and a lion to frighten off wolves."

Is that governance, then? Abdicating one's humanity to act like an animal and wear the skin of a wild beast? Is *The Prince* no more than that? A pitiful collection of tricks that boils down to a knack for dissimulation and a carnival pleasure in dressing up? The trap is in getting upset over this. Let us calmly pick up where we stopped earlier, at this general piece of advice in Chapter 15:

> Hence it is necessary for a prince who wishes to maintain his position to learn how to be able not to be good, and to use or not use this ability according to need.

That says it all, in a few words. Need: Machiavelli's political philosophy is a philosophy of necessity. It has a single aim: self-preservation. His rules of action have no other end than their utility: use them or not according to necessity. He cautions against always being harsh: in a later passage, he writes that it is inadvisable for a prince to arouse the envy of his people by taking up quarters in a sumptuous or forbidding palace, since the best fortress of all is not to be hated by one's people. No uncalled-for cruelty, therefore, no unbridled violence. A prince should make measured use of force — in short, learn how to be able not to be good.

I freely concede that Machiavelli has never looked more like the caricature of himself promoted by his outraged adversaries. But his thinking here is far more subversive than the run-of-the-mill amorality of the cynics. To Machiavelli, the question of good or evil is essentially adverbial: the prince is not called on to do good or evil; he does well or ill what he has to do.

And what does he have to deal with? Mainly the baseness of man. Of course, it is best to be both loved and feared by those one governs. But if you must choose between the two, says the author of *The Prince*, make yourself feared:

> For one can make this generalization about men: they are ungrateful, fickle, liars, and deceivers, they shun danger and are greedy for profit; while you treat them well, they are yours. They would shed their blood for

you, risk their property, their lives, their sons, so long, as I said above, as danger is remote; but when you are in danger, they turn away.

Are we shocked to hear this? Would we rather be governed by statesmen who assure us, hand on heart, that they truly love us? That might be the wrong choice. Because again, if we make an effort to suspend all moral judgment, what Machiavelli says is very simple: the prince must always put himself in the position of expecting the worst from those he governs. Today's legislators know this well, or they should: you don't make laws hoping they will be followed in a virtuous and disinterested way. You make laws, or avoid making them, anticipating their most nefarious use.

Still from *Ivan the Terrible*

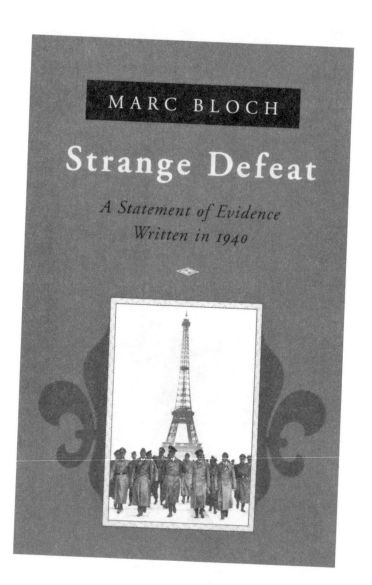

Marc Bloch, *Strange Defeat*

FIFTEEN

STATE OF EMERGENCY

HISTORIANS RARELY PROVE TO HAVE a very lucid view of the present. For the most part, neither their methods nor their knowledge prevent them from being blinded. The only exception, or very nearly, is the French historian Marc Bloch. His *Strange Defeat*, written in the white-hot heat of events in 1940, implacably describes the moral and intellectual crisis of the French governing classes, which led to the fall of France when Germany invaded. This great work of immediate history was also a call to resistance. It was published two years after the Nazis tortured and executed Marc Bloch on June 16, 1944.

With *The Prince*, Machiavelli composed his own *Strange Defeat*, in a certain sense. The defeat was that of the Italian princes who were unable to maintain their states before the *furia francese* of the French armies from across the mountains who had been strewing havoc in their path since 1494. And he didn't want to hear about bad luck! Fortune can be capricious, of course:

I compare fortune to one of those violent rivers which,

when they are enraged, flood the plains, tear down trees
and buildings, wash soil from one place to deposit it in
another. Everyone flees before them, everyone yields
to their impetus, there is no possibility of resistance.

Then what's to be done? Why, what engineers do,
Leonardo da Vinci and the rest. He has seen them at
work, Machiavelli, he has accompanied them onto the
construction sites where they altered the course of the
Arno. He has seen them divert channels, build embank-
ments, empondments, outlets, releases — in a word, he
has watched them govern, which is to act upon adverse
events. But it takes a certain *virtù* to do so, a political virtue
that is also a form of practical reason, a virtue that Machiavelli despairs of ever teaching the princes of his era.

The last three chapters of *The Prince* strike a note of
urgent and painful exhortation. The time is past for Machiavelli to alternate reassuringly, as Plutarch did in his *Lives*,
between examples from the history of ancient Rome and
contemporary experience of the world. Like a river over-
flowing its banks, Machiavelli's anxiety about present
times carries everything in its path — including, appar-
ently, his republican convictions. In the end, he appeals
to the unalloyed power of a modern prince to deliver Italy
from "the stench of this barbarian dominion."

"Stench," and "barbarians"; those are the terms Machiavelli uses to speak of the French in the last chapter of *The
Prince*, abandoning any ironic distance and showing a previously undisclosed patriotic strain. *Italia mia*, he quotes

from Petrarch, and we realize that this poetic glorification of Italy is, as it were, the expression of a wounded identity, showing that Machiavelli would willingly consent to the use of force and authoritarian power.

With this, we are certainly entering a dangerous zone, perhaps justified by the state of emergency in which Machiavelli wrote. He justifies the use of force and authority, and he incites their use at the same time — in the manner of those societies that become violent for lack of anything better to do. Machiavelli is unquestionably desperate to get back in the game, to seduce Fortune, for this river is also a woman whom one must know how to win over. Writing, writing, always writing — when will he finally be loved?

Leonardo da Vinci, *The Arno Valley*

POLITICS OF
WRITING

Leonardo da Vinci, *Map of the Arno River*, 1504

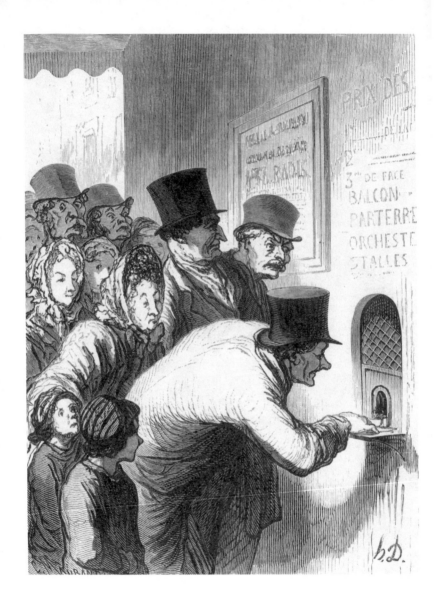

Charles Maurand after Honoré Daumier, *Box Office*

SIXTEEN

THE COMEDY OF POWER

SO THE WHOLE THING was a bust. If Machiavelli's intention in writing *The Prince* was to show how indispensable a man of his mettle was in ensuring the preservation of the state, he manifestly failed. The book did not go unnoticed, and Niccolò Machiavelli harbored some hope in 1514 that he might return to favor. But this hope was quickly squelched. In a letter written in February 1515, Pope Leo X cautioned Giuliano de' Medici "not to compromise himself with Niccolò." While the threat of a major French offensive was coming to a head (1515: Battle of Marignano), it was the pope who was dictating Florence's politics.

The struggle would have to continue, but in another theater of operations. The theater...and why not? Machiavelli had always had a liking for the satiric comedies of ancient Rome. As a young man, he had tried to translate Terence and written a first play, whose title alone survives: *The Masks*.

In 1520, another of his comedies was performed in Florence, one that was probably written a few years earlier. "This play is called *The Mandrake*," we learn from the prologue. "The playwright is not of any great renown, but he will stand you a glass of wine if he cannot make you laugh."

He wouldn't need to. The play was an instant success. When it was performed at a convent in Venice two years later, the public was so enthusiastic that the play had to be stopped. A bitter revenge for the author of *The Prince*, who, again in the prologue, asks our indulgence for presenting such frivolous material:

> Excuse him in this: that he is trying his utmost to lighten his misery, for he has nowhere else to turn, barred as he is from demonstrating his skills and abilities through worthier tasks, his labor no longer prized.

The plot of *The Mandrake* may indeed appear slight: a dim-witted, elderly husband, Nicia, is gulled by the stratagems of Callimaco, who has set his sights on seducing Lucrezia, Nicia's lovely young wife. Also present are a crafty counselor and a hypocritical friar named Timoteo, who complete the picture of a corrupt society contaminated by the poisonous mandrake plant.

Should we read this as a political allegory, with Friar Timoteo as Savonarola and Lucrezia as Florence? Is the senile republic being robbed of its young wife, who has been seduced by the appealing tyranny of the Medici? Perhaps. But the most political aspect of this comedy, more even than any possible hidden meaning, is the drama itself. That is, the fact that Machiavelli has applied to a lighthearted intrigue the implacable workings of the passions and interests that underlie *The Prince*, in an obsessively disillusioned world where everyone seems to speak in maxims.

Love, in short, is the pursuit of war by the same means. The campaign to win Lucrezia is methodically conducted, following a sequence of stratagems that she, at first shy and modest, coldly consents to when she realizes that it is always better to adapt to the quality of the times. The action takes place in a deadened world, as though Florence were tense and paralyzed with fear: "Do you think the Turks will invade Italy this year?" a character asks, adding "I am horribly afraid of their custom of impaling everyone."

Is this truly a comedy? Yes, if a comedy can be about laughing at one's own despair.

ENCYCLOPÉDIE,

OU

DICTIONNAIRE RAISONNÉ

DES SCIENCES,

DES ARTS ET DES MÉTIERS,

PAR UNE SOCIÉTÉ DE GENS DE LETTRES.

Mis en ordre & publié par M. *DIDEROT*, de l'Académie Royale des Sciences & des Belles-Lettres de Prusse ; & quant à la PARTIE MATHÉMATIQUE, par M. *D'ALEMBERT*, de l'Académie Royale des Sciences de Paris, de celle de Prusse, & de la Société Royale de Londres.

Tantùm series juncturaque pollet,
Tantùm de medio sumptis accedit honoris ! HORAT.

TOME PREMIER.

A PARIS,

Chez
{
BRIASSON, *rue Saint Jacques, à la Science.*
DAVID l'aîné, *rue Saint Jacques, à la Plume d'or.*
LE BRETON, Imprimeur ordinaire du Roy, *rue de la Harpe.*
DURAND, *rue Saint Jacques, à Saint Landry, & au Griffon.*
}

M. DCC. LI.

AVEC APPROBATION ET PRIVILEGE DU ROY.

Title page from Diderot, *Encyclopédie*

SEVENTEEN

MACHIAVELLI THE JOKER

"HISTORIAN, AUTHOR OF COMIC AND TRAGIC WORKS." So Machiavelli described himself at the end of his life, in a letter to his friend Guicciardini. He most likely never wrote tragedies, but he used his comic plays — *The Mandrake* and, later, *Clizia* — to express, paradoxically, his tragic sense of history. Clearly, he identified as a man of letters, because he was always addressing an audience, either readers or spectators.

Once the importance of theater in the works of Machiavelli has been realized, the whole of his writings takes on a theatrical aspect. If you reread *The Prince* after reading *The Mandrake*, you not only find the same themes of dissimulation, pretence, and outward appearance but come to understand that a powerful, imperious theatrical energy runs through the text.

And, in fact, the text has been presented on the stage, since Machiavelli distributes his roles like the characters in a plot. It would be pointless to try to identify which voice utters the author's own political convictions. Each voice plays its part, and the reality of the drama lies in the tension created when different perspectives clash. This would explain why Machiavelli speaks in a variety of modes, shifting from the familiar form of address to the formal in dialoguing with his reader or prince. And was it not in the form of a dialogue that political treatises were originally written? In this case, it is a dialogue that changes genres as well as voices, abruptly swerving in tone, with laughter suddenly erupting in the midst of a historical drama — an effect that almost seems Shakespearian, to introduce an anachronism.

Recognizing the theatricality, the reader is assailed by doubts. What if Machiavelli was joking? In the article on Machiavellianism in Diderot's *Encyclopédie*, we find this intriguing comment: "His contemporaries were at fault for mistaking his purpose: they read as praise what was intended as satire." Nothing is harder to perceive than the subtle art of joyful provocation. When he embarks with apparent relish, in Chapter 8 of *The Prince*, on a distinction between "well used and badly used cruelty" in the actions of the ancient tyrant Agathocles, king of Sicily, and of Cesare Borgia, his contemporary, perhaps Machiavelli is perpetrating a caricature so broad that it amounts to a proof by absurdity.

In a letter to his friend Francesco Vettori dated January 31, 1515, he writes:

If anyone were to read our letters, most honorable friend, he would be highly surprised at their diversity, for he would find that at one moment we are sober, serious men, engaging in important matters, and that our minds could have only large and honest thoughts. But on turning the page, he would find that we are shallow, changeable, lascivious, and absorbed in vain topics. While this manner of behaving may strike some as shameful, I believe it to be praiseworthy, for we are imitating nature, which is variable.

Varietas is the key word. We should be diverse, varied, undisciplined — at the same time sad and cheerful, so as not to despair of the business of living.

Leonardo da Vinci, *Three Heads of a Man*

Auguste Belloc, *Nude Woman*

EIGHTEEN

POLITICS OF OBSCENITY

BUT I'M FALLING SHORT OF MY DUTIES. I haven't introduced you to his romantic life. Machiavelli talked about it often, straightforwardly, with a disarming mix of tenderness and obscenity. Shortly after his father's death, he married the woman who would remain his wife throughout his life. It was in the summer of 1501, and her name was Marietta Corsini. She came from a noble but impecunious family. He wrote to her from time to time, though not often enough, in her opinion, especially when he was called on by the Florentine Republic to travel on endless missions. "I would be grateful if you would write me a little more often, as I have only received three letters since your departure." (This letter, dated November 1503, is the only extant letter from Marietta to Niccolò Machiavelli.) She continued: "The baby is in good health at the moment, and he looks like you: his skin is as fair as snow, but his head seems covered in black velvet, and he is as hairy as you. As he resembles you, I find him handsome."

The child Marietta refers to was their son, the eldest of their five children, named Bernardo after Niccolò's father. Until his own death, Machiavelli wrote him attentive letters, just as he wrote to Bernardo's brothers and sisters. No doubt, he was intent on maintaining a large and flourishing household around his wife. Yet we don't necessarily have to believe him when, in 1525, in the prologue to his play *Clizia*, where an older man engages in love play with some young and frisky women, he writes:

> I should add that the author of this play is a man of upright morals, and it would pain him if, in watching the action, you should find anything crude or off-color.

Ten years earlier, he had experienced a romance that had consoled him for his exile and his disappointments in the world of politics. To a friend, he wrote:

> Let me just say that although I am approaching fifty, the sun's rays do not vex me, nor rough roads tire me, nor does the darkness of night frighten me. Everything now seems effortless, and I adapt myself to all her whims, no matter how contrary they might be to my disposition. Even though I sense I am courting great trouble I feel much sweetness, because of how her rare and gracious countenance transports me, and because it has cast aside all thoughts of my many predicaments, so that I would not want to free myself for anything in the world, even if I could.

The tone is all the more surprising in that it avoids the ribaldry Machiavelli normally used in his letters when telling of his amorous adventures. One letter, dating from 1509, is so scabrous that I hesitate to quote it here. Written from Verona to his friend Luigi Guicciardini, it describes his "desperate rut" with an old and atrociously ugly prostitute.

No doubt Machiavelli's harrowing description harks back to the literature of derision that he had such fondness for. He brings in all the narrative elements — bestiality, deformity, and lust — that add hilarity to bitterness. To present obscenity is to make visible what normally occurs out of sight, but it's also to play the bearer of bad tidings. Machiavelli is definitely an unsavory character. But the reason we so like to detest him is that he is quick to cop to his unsavoriness.

René Magritte, *The Key to Dreams*

NINETEEN

THE COURAGE TO NAME

AS HIS FRIENDS DROPPED AWAY, Machiavelli's correspondence gradually tapered off, and while the events in his life can be followed day by day during the period of his intense political activity — the fifteen years, from 1498 to 1512, during which he was "neither nodding off nor wasting time" — his life now was marked only by his writing. The exact sequence of his works has not, however, been determined with certainty. The one sure thing is that from this point on he never stopped writing, putting his hand to every genre and moving nimbly from one to another. Poetry, drama, treatises, moral philosophy, history: all were good as long as they allowed him to practice the art of the mot juste, which the meanness of the times demanded. For when only an uncertain relation exists between words and things, when an unjust power is at work undermining the language of politics, the need for literature is greatest. And not only to set the calm and solemn power of books in opposition to the malignancies of fortune, but to draw from them the courage to name.

And in what does naming consist? In pointing out,

in finding the exact word, the one that brings you back to the truth of the thing itself, not the common idea of it. And to do that, you need to renew the language. In France, the language of power was widely recognized after 1968 as having become outdated. Not only was the language of political cant heavy and repetitive, but it also sought to hide an inability or unwillingness to say things; it manipulated empty words, scrupulously avoiding direct reference.

The task at hand is to take back one by one all the words that have been stolen, wrung of their meaning from having been turned this way and that, and to reenergize them, restore the joyous energy that comes from their density — I almost said their explosiveness. A poetic and political renewal, then, the two being inseparably entwined. This is the work that Machiavelli performs on the language of his day. He restricts himself to ordinary language and avoids neologisms, using a spare form of Latin. When he writes *stato* in *The Prince*, a word he uses 116 times, he deftly rings the changes on all its many possible meanings (power, domination, territory, government . . .) and keeps the word's capacity to designate on high alert.

In this, Machiavelli conforms to the diplomatic language of his time, but augmented: his Italian is the idiom of the chancery and the tavern, of elevated poetry and coarse humor. He defended the dignity of the Tuscan dialect in a discourse inspired by Dante, whose work he passionately admired. This didn't prevent him from parodying the *Divina Commedia* in a burlesque philosophical poem called *The Golden Ass*. It was probably during the same decade, the 1510s, that he imitated the narrative style of Boccacio in a short story called "Belfagor."

Did he truly intend to rival the greatest Italian writers of his day? Possibly, to judge from a letter Machiavelli wrote to a friend of Ariosto, the celebrated author of *Orlando Furioso*:

> If you see him, please pass on my greetings and tell him that my one complaint is that, having cited so many poets, he ignored me *come un cazzo*, like a turd.

The courage to name, as I've said. Hasn't it been claimed that the function of a writer is to call a cat a cat?

Riverside Shakespeare Company production of *The Mandrake*

Paolo Veronese, *Three Archers* (detail)

TWENTY

THE POLITICAL ART OF TAKING A POSITION

DO YOU WISH TO REACH THE GOAL that you've set for your-self? Then follow the lead of the experienced archer. He sights at a spot above his target, not to shoot beyond it but to hit it. In other words, aim high to aim accurately. The metaphor comes from classical rhetoric, and Machiavelli drew on it to justify using "very great examples" of famous men as guides to action in his political works, and notably in *The Prince*. When it comes to political language, education, or simply the way we conduct our lives, we should remember this lesson: that to propose lofty examples is not to be presumptuous about our abilities but rather, as Machiavelli writes, "to know how far the strength of our bow carries."

The marksman and the painter both have to develop the art of taking a position. Finding the right angle, moving if necessary to one side or another, but facing one's objective without wavering. This is an eminently political art, hence Machiavelli's frequent allusions to it, as in this striking passage from the dedication to *The Prince*:

> Just as men who are sketching the landscape put them-
> selves down in the plain to study the nature of the
> mountains and the highlands, and to study the low-
> lying land they put themselves high on the mountains,
> so, to comprehend fully the nature of the people, one
> must be a prince, and to comprehend fully the nature
> of princes one must be an ordinary citizen.

"Just as ..." This is the language of comparison. But
with whom? "Men who are sketching the landscape"
could be either cartographers or painters. Leonardo da
Vinci was both, and he tried to bring harmony to the
rhythms of the world by his obstinate drawing. Making visible the quality of the times: in this, Leonardo and
Machiavelli were contemporaries, and not only because
they very probably met, in the years 1502 to 1504, in
Romagna at the court of Cesare Borgia, in Florence in
the Palazzo della Signoria, and elsewhere in Tuscany on
construction sites when a deviation was planned in the
course of the Arno River.

There, in the lands below, is the best position from
which to understand the art of government. No doubt
there exists a science of the state known to princes and
those who advise them. They grasp the nature of the
ordinary citizen, which is to say that they observe, from
above, the social passions motivating them. But what
they don't see, from their elevated position, is the reality of their own power. Those who understand it best,

in fact, are those subjected to it. What Machiavelli willingly concedes to those who are dominated is the knowledge of their domination. And this knowledge is strongly liberating to those willing to share it. As he writes in his *Discourses on the First Ten Books of Titus Livius*: the people know what is oppressing them.

What is this book of Machiavelli's, the *Discourses*, and in what does the political science of disagreement consist? That is what we will try to understand going forward. But let us not forget the point of this visual metaphor for political knowledge. It doesn't distance us from the portrait of Machiavelli as a man of letters, a writer, and a creative soul. Rather, it brings us closer. Because it reminds us that to expose the true nature of the thing itself, you must in some sense invent it.

REPUBLIC OF DISAGREEMENTS

Gardens of the Palazzo Rucellai

TWENTY-ONE

WHAT IS A REPUBLIC?

IMAGINE A SMALL GARDEN in the shade of a palazzo. People come here to take the air, under the classical statues and the fragrant trees, whose exotic species suggest the vastness of the world. The talk is of literature and politics, perhaps as a break from refined conversation, but also perhaps to pave the way for the future. What people are we talking about? A few highborn men of Florence, gathered around Cosimo Rucellai, the master of these precincts, known in Latin as the Orti Oricellari, the gardens of the Palazzo Rucellai.

Have I mentioned that Machiavelli was a wonderful talker? He was. So much so that, starting in 1517, many came to hear him discourse on the Roman republic. In the first century of the Christian era, Livy had written about its origins in his massive *History of Rome*. No one expected Machiavelli to produce a soberly ordered exegesis of the classical scholar, an academic exercise. He combed Livy's work for rules of action. Proceeding with full freedom, he tried to correct the present using the intelligence of the past.

It's likely that Machiavelli was returning to a field he had first started to explore even before writing *The Prince*. His *Discourses on the First Ten Books of Titus Livius*, as this unfinished work came to be known, was only published in 1532, five years after its author's death. Was it a counterbalance to *The Prince* in the republican vein? In a sense yes, the two works echo each other. The *Discourses* comprises three parts of unequal length; its thesis is wandering and disjointed. If *The Prince* was taut, focused, and cutting, the *Discourses* teems with ideas, which it sets forth ramblingly. Its editors were hard put to bring coherence to this shifting mass, which seems buffeted by history, or rather by Machiavelli's energetic attempt to derive from the materials of history a practical art of freedom.

Naturally you find brilliant passages on republican government in the *Discourses*. But in the end, the book is less attentive to the workings of republican institutions than to the idea of popular sovereignty itself. Recognizing its legitimacy, which is the basis of every republic, entails a political anthropology of the nature of man. This is what Machiavelli is after.

Book I, Chapter 58 is entitled "On How the Populace Is Wiser and More Constant Than the Prince." Here is a taste of it:

It is not without reason that the voice of the people has been compared to the voice of God. One sees public opinion making surprising prognostications, so that it seems that the populace, as if by some hidden skill, can foresee their good and bad fortune.

This is the primary tenet of the republican faith. As Machiavelli's text continues, it progressively weakens the argument, presenting many historical examples of the populace being wrong — and worse, of the populace being deceived by the most bald-faced lies. Whence the crucial statement made in Chapter 47:

Men make mistakes in their overall judgments, but they don't make mistakes about the details.

What is the populace? An opinion. Is this opinion well-founded? No, generally it is mistaken. Why is it mistaken? Because the populace generally sees things from a distance. What is a republic? The form of government that takes account of this opinion, even when it consists of emotions and prejudices. So how can you continue as a republican? By allowing the populace to draw close to the reality of power, so that it can see things close-up and not be fooled by general ideas.

"Theory of the Four Humors"

TWENTY-TWO

IN PRAISE OF DISAGREEMENT

COME NOW, BE REASONABLE, you haven't been listening. The moralists, from the Stoics to the humanists, from Seneca to Petrarch, have all been saying it: the multitude is a noisy and ignorant monster. How can the people govern themselves?

The populace can govern, says Machiavelli in his *Discourses on the First Ten Books of Titus Livius*, because although ignorant it is capable of truth. The people know what they want, or, more accurately, they know what they don't want: to be dominated. Through this knowledge, the people arrive at the truth, which is the truth of domination.

The idea makes an early appearance in Chapter 9 of *The Prince*:

> In every city there are two opposing humors; this arises from the fact that the nobles want to command and oppress the people, but the people do not want to be commanded or oppressed by the nobles.

Where Machiavelli talks about opposing humors, we

might use the term "social aspirations." But Machiavelli's use of "humors" draws on a metaphor from Hippocratic medicine.

According to Hippocrates, a person's health was dependent on his bodily fluids being in balance. The physician's art lies in maintaining that balance. And, like medicine, the art of politics is a science that deals with singularities and consists of making diagnoses. Machiavelli's diagnosis can be found in the *Discourses*: the health of the body politic results from the proper balance of its humors. The political order consists in organizing social conflicts, not papering them over. In other words, the republic is based on discord; it is the peaceful and equilibrial arrangement of disagreement.

There's more — more troubling, I mean, and more scandalous. You think that good laws are the creations of virtuous legislators? Then you are still an idealist. No, just laws come from putting to good use this original social conflict. "All the laws that are passed in favor of freedom," wrote Machiavelli, "arise from the discord" of these two humors. When he attributed Rome's greatness to the divide between the people and the Senate, Machiavelli was as usual being an incorrigible provocateur. He knew that the Florentines hated dissension and feared turmoil. But he also knew that the wisdom of the ancient Romans was in having imparted order to that conflict, orchestrated the clash of wills.

That is what politics comes to: seeing that there is orderliness among the people. Because a free life, an authentically free life, is regulated by law — that is, a constraining norm that is recognized by all. What is most damaging to the public spirit, Machiavelli wrote, is "to make a law and not observe it, particularly when it is not observed by the person who devised it."

But the author of the *Discourses* is not without a favorite between the dominant and the dominated. In Book I, Chapter 58, we read:

> The cruelty of the populace is directed against those whom the populace fears will seize public property, while the cruelty of the prince is directed against those he fears will take his property.

Accepting the principle of symmetry between the two humors is already to take the people's point of view, recognizing that its motivation is the love of justice. Has Machiavelli suddenly become an idealist? Not at all; in fact he is approaching a dangerous zone, where history turns to violence.

Leonardo da Vinci, *Head of a Warrior*

TWENTY-THREE

WE ARE DISARMED

LET'S GO DOWN INTO THE GARDEN AGAIN, if you're willing. The garden of the Rucellai, where Machiavelli discussed ancient literature and modern politics with ambitious Florentine patricians. It was in this garden that our author situated the fictional dialogue of his *Art of War*, which pits a condottiere, the commander of a troop of mercenaries, against an aristocrat on the subject of how the Roman legions were organized and on the need to make a complete overhaul of modern warfare along those lines. This treatise, published in 1521, was the only political work Machiavelli published in his lifetime. Its thinking is archaeological (there is a learned dissertation on the military strategy of the ancient Romans), technical (there are tactical plans for the movement of troops), and above all political.

To Machiavelli, the question of military force was crucial to the preservation of the state. And the state was defined first and foremost by its response to a fundamental choice: What portions of its population will bear arms, and what portions will remain without arms? Today we might say: How are we to distribute the recourse to legitimate violence?

On this point, Machiavelli has long held a firm conviction. It is unambiguously expressed in *The Prince*:

> The present ruin of Italy has been caused by nothing else but a reliance on mercenary armies for a period of many years.

Heroes of fortune, committed to nothing and ready for anything, these military entrepreneurs were paid to make war, and paid even more to avoid war. In Italy, they were called "condottieri," because they signed a contract, a *condotta*, with the state, which didn't stop them from betraying it at the first opportunity to offer their services to a higher bidder.

This description is no doubt exaggerated, as Italian states in the fifteenth century managed to discipline their condottieri's troops. But these mercenaries were no match for the permanent armies of the large national monarchies. And they broke with a political principle Machiavelli was constantly repeating:

> The best of all armies are those that consist of armed citizens.

This was his main battle in life, and it was anything but theoretical. In 1509, he had raised a civic militia in Florence, and he defended its military and political effectiveness until the day he died.

Was it his aim to imitate the legionaries of a staunch and virtuous Rome? It is no doubt true that he based his concept of the modern army on antiquity. But Machiavelli also took stock of contemporary examples. The Swiss, because they were "the only ones to preserve a semblance of the militia of ancient Rome," were "the masters of modern war." It was true that in the 1510s, the armies of Switzerland determined the political situation in Italy. But what Machiavelli admired most about them was the political cohesion of their peasant soldiers, united in defense of their cantons' freedom.

His detractors mocked Machiavelli as an armchair strategist, ignorant of the power of artillery, who fantasized about bringing back the discipline of an imagined antiquity. They were wrong. Machiavelli was the first theoretician of dirty warfare, a brutal and political warfare enlisting partisans, whose military campaigns would be "big and short" — which is to say, massive in scale and lightning quick. He imagined battle as the paroxysmal encounter of armed forces. His thinking was eminently practical and at the same time deeply disturbing, as it put violence at the heart of political decisions. We'd much rather do without it. But is this a choice we can make?

Flemish, *The Battle of Pavia* (detail)

TWENTY-FOUR

VIOLENCE IN POLITICS

THE ART OF WAR ends on a cruel and ironic note:

> Our Italian princes believed that it was enough for
> them, sitting in their private chambers, to summon up
> a brilliant response, to compose a good letter, to dis-
> play subtlety and perspicacity in their utterances, to
> know how to detect a trick, to adorn themselves with
> gold and jewels, to sleep and eat more sumptuously
> than everyone else ...

And all to protect themselves from the vicissitudes of
fortune. Poor princes. They never saw what was coming: "great terrors, sudden collapses, and formidable
disasters."

Thus, if there was a Renaissance in Italy, or, as we
would put it crudely today, an over-investment in the cultural production industry, it was because princes thought
that to invest their energy in that quarter was not a dis-
traction from the baubles of power but a way to exercise
that power effectively. In other words, to provide a beau-
tiful setting for power was to provide for its defense —

you protect yourself with a screen of flattering intellects and lovely objects.

This is a consoling idea and an attractive one. The thought can only gratify us. But it shatters into a thousand pieces at the shrill Machiavellian laugh that greets it, bringing us back to reality. A wise ruler, we learn in *The Prince*, "should work toward no purpose and think about no subject other than war, its institutions, and its science." But what then is peace? Machiavelli answers: it is violence in abeyance, violence of the kind that doesn't need to be used except as an insidious deterrent, all the more effective for being kept vague, shifting, and unspecified.

The state's hidden hand is revealed in certain circumstances: when a coup d'état is attempted. The *Discourses on the First Ten Books of Titus Livius* give a description of this in a little treatise within the treatise, which has often since been published on its own. Drawing on a broad palette of historical examples, Machiavelli first shows that what is most dangerous for a prince is a plot hatched by those closest to him:

> A prince who would protect himself against plots therefore has more to fear from those he has greatly benefited than from those he has greatly harmed.

He goes on to demonstrate that conspiracies generally fail, that they are most dangerous to those who foment them, and that they are an unavailing form of political struggle.

Coups strengthen the state they are meant to undermine. And yet — pay close attention here, because Machiavelli has in typical fashion thought several moves ahead — in making itself stronger, the state makes itself weaker. Machiavelli describes this in his *History of Florence*:

> As a result, when in such a conspiracy a prince is attacked and is not killed (as most often happens), the prince emerges with greater power, and frequently, even if he was a good man before the conspiracy, will turn evil. This happens because conspiracies give the prince reason to fear, and fear gives him reason to secure himself, and securing himself gives him reason to harm others, from which arises hatred and, often enough, the prince's ruin. Hence these conspiracies quickly crush those who conspire, while those who are conspired against will with time inevitably cause harm.

A final twist from a thinker known to have a taste for paradox? It goes deeper than that: coups reveal what states normally keep hidden, which is their constituent violence, the violence kept in reserve in the conduct of government. But as soon as it is revealed, its strength diminishes. It remains powerful only while it is indeterminate. All the more reason to say, as Machiavelli does: the king is naked.

Antoinette Bouzonnet-Stella, *Discovery of Romulus and Remus*

TWENTY-FIVE

THE END DOES NOT JUSTIFY THE MEANS

THE STORY IS ABOUT A MAN who murders his brother. He kills him horribly for the simple reason that he doesn't want to share power with him. Alone, he founds a city, and that city becomes the capital of the greatest empire in history. The city is Rome, the murderer is Romulus, and the victim, who was suckled by a she-wolf alongside his twin brother, is Remus. You know the story of this founding crime, but how does one make sense of it? How can we accept that a country should become great at the cost of original murder?

In the Roman tradition, and in the Christian tradition as well, the interpretation of this fratricide has fallen into two main camps. The first, notably represented by Livy, minimizes the crime; the second dramatizes it. Cicero, for example, puts the brother-killing at the origin of every civil war. Among the later Christian authors, such as Augustine, it becomes the original sin behind every political structure.

And Machiavelli? Characteristically, he addresses the awkward question head-on, this being the prime instance of foundational violence. In his *Discourses on the First Ten Books of Titus Livius*, he takes issue with both traditions:

> Many might judge it a bad example that a founder of a state, such as Romulus, would first have killed his brother.

But if Romulus perpetrated violence, it was "for the sake of reconciliation" rather than "for the sake of destruction." He wanted "not to benefit himself but rather the people, not his own heirs but his whole state." We must therefore agree to the following proposition: "While his actions might accuse him, the result excuses him."

Did you hear that? He finally came out with it! Those famous words that sum up his doctrine in the minds of anti-Machiavellians: to excuse Romulus when the facts accuse him is to admit that the end justifies the means. But, in fact, it is more subtle. Machiavelli is writing in the future perfect tense: the founding of Rome absolves Romulus of his crime, but it does so after the fact. Romulus did not have the right to kill his brother, but he will have earned the right to do it once the beneficial effect of his action has been demonstrated. Which means that the state is not in the right when it is rightfully founded. It sits on the blurred threshold between force and law, where what has the force of law draws authority from something outside itself, from the exception it makes for original violence. One can therefore condemn the founder's violence and recognize the legitimacy of what he has founded.

All the same, this doesn't mean that the end justifies the means. Machiavelli never wrote those words, nor would he have been capable of it. His philosophy of necessity rests on the principle of the changeableness of the times and the unpredictability of political action. It would be impossible for the means to justify the end, since, at the moment one is acting, the end is still unknown. The end will always occur too late to justify the means of an action. To govern is to act blindly within the indeterminacy of the times. The moral is frightening: that is why this start, the founding murder of Remus by Romulus, still stands today.

NEVER
TOO LATE

Giuseppe Lorenzo Gatteri, *The Tumult of the Ciompi*

Sebastiano del Piombo, *Portrait of Pope Clement VII*

TWENTY-SIX

WRITING HISTORY

ON MAY 4, 1519, Lorenzo de' Medici died at the age of twenty-seven. He spent most of his short life frustrating the political expectations he had raised. Machiavelli dedicated *The Prince* to him, but in vain. Now that he was gone, things could move forward. Pope Leo X picked his cousin Cardinal Giulio de' Medici to take over the government of Florence. Again a Medici, but this one a man you could deal with.

After knocking on the doors of the powerful for a long time, Machiavelli finally was offered something. In 1520, the members of the Florentine Academy voted to commission him to write a history of Florence. It was to be completed in two years and written in Latin or the vulgar tongue, as he chose, for the price of fifty-seven gold florins, not a penny more. Take it or leave it.

He took it. So Machiavelli was now a public historian, responsible for the official chronicle of a city, or rather of the family that loomed over it, the Medici. Was he prepared to do anything to reenter politics, to the point of becoming the incense bearer for those who brought down the Republic of Florence? No, not a chance. He was planning to be devious, as he wrote his friend Guicciardini on May 17, 1521:

> For some time now, I have no longer said what I think, nor do I ever think what I say. If sometimes I tell the truth, I hide it among so many lies that it is hard to find.

How are we to find the truth of this *History of Florence*, then, which Machiavelli completed in four years, finally, and in Italian? More than an exercise in duplicity, it was a way of cutting down to size the great and the good. Machiavelli saw the writing of history as an opportunity to be disagreeable. With his patrons, of course, but also with those expecting him to call those patrons to account for their shortcomings. What drives his narrative is the urge to disillusion. He neither glorifies great men nor waxes eloquent over principles, neither fawns like a courtier nor preens like a virtuous orator.

No, when Machiavelli writes history, he means to describe the full extent of the strife, the discord, the enmity that played out in his city's politics. The most famous passage in the *History of Florence* is about the Revolt of the Ciompi. It occurred during the summer of 1378 and brought the *ciompi*, or wool carders, and other low-wage workers in Florence's thriving wool industry to power. The patrician class was so shaken that the effects of the rebellion were still felt 150 years later.

Machiavelli accurately assessed the fear of those in

power, as this speech by one of the rioters who favored political violence shows:

> I believe that our rebellion will surely be successful, because those who oppose it are rich and divided among themselves. Their lack of unity will give us the victory, and their riches, once we have seized them, will allow us to remain in control. The fact that they can trace their origins to ancient times is nothing to be afraid of. For all men share the same origins, are equally ancient, and are made by nature in the same way. Let every one of you strip off his clothes, and you will see that we are all alike. If we then get dressed in their clothes and they in ours, we will certainly appear noble, and they will not.

This passage was long read as a manifesto, a subversive screed, as though the rebellious workman spoke for Machiavelli. But putting fine speeches in the mouths of historical characters plays no part in writing history. It consists here in giving equal dignity to the *ciompi* and the Medici, in giving those who have no voice a hearing, in saying in plain terms that this took place, this was possible.

Rio dei Mendicanti and the Scuola Grande di San Marco

TWENTY-SEVEN

IS IT TOO LATE?

HE WAS ON THE WAY BACK. No, he was on the rise. On March 17, 1520, one of his politically connected friends, Filippo Strozzi, wrote to his brother Lorenzo, to whom *The Art of War* was dedicated:

> I'm glad you were able to bring Machiavelli to visit the Medici, because as long as he manages to win the confidence of our masters somewhat, he is a man on the rise.

Would Niccolò Machiavelli make up for lost time? For eight years he had been writing in exile, and now he was back on the road to political action. At first his missions were modest, in keeping with the degree of confidence he inspired. He traveled to Lucca to settle a business matter, to Carpi to negotiate with the Friars Minor of Tuscany. Then in November 1523, Cardinal Giulio de' Medici, for whom Machiavelli was writing his *History of Florence*, was elevated to the papacy as Pope Clement VII. His sphere of action grew, and Machiavelli began conducting embassies to Venice and Rome.

But in the meantime, matters in Italy had taken a drastic turn. The Italian Wars had entered their second phase, broadening out into Europe and bringing into conflict the two great sovereigns with universalist pretensions, King Francis I of France and Charles V, heir to the House of Habsburg, the Burgundian territories, and the Kingdom of Naples, who also ruled Spain and the Holy Roman Empire. On February 24, 1525, Charles inflicted a disastrous defeat on Francis I at the Battle of Pavia, while the peasants in Germany, energized by the Lutheran Reformation, rose up in rebellion.

History was occurring on a grand scale. What could the little Italian states do to keep from being buffeted in its impetuous current? Fortune is like a river in spate. In June 1526, Machiavelli went to the camp in Lombardy where the armies of the League of Cognac were gathering in opposition to the imperial forces. The league included Venice, Florence, Milan, Francis I, and the pope. Machiavelli took up military life again: he came to know the young and brilliant condottiere Giovanni dalle Bande Nere and renewed contact with Francesco Guicciardini, lieutenant general of the papal army.

For several years, Machiavelli had engaged in an extensive correspondence with Guicciardini. "More than anyone," the latter wrote to his friend, "you have kept your distance from the common wisdom and invented new and unusual ideas." Was it too late? Too late for action, perhaps. Machiavelli had given up on the Republic of Florence and the possibility that the Italians might defend themselves against the imperial armies. But it is never too late to make an assessment of the times and ward off disaster, never too late to organize a response, never too late to devote oneself to the politics of friendship.

What is history, and can it reoccur? Here is Guicciardini writing in the affectionate and bantering tone he used in addressing his friend:

My dear Machiavelli, I earnestly believe that only men's faces and the outward aspect of things change, while the same things reoccur again and again. Thus we are witnessing events that happened earlier. But the alteration in names and outward aspects is such that only the most learned are able to recognize them. That is why history is a useful and profitable discipline, because it shows you and allows you to recognize what you've never seen or experienced.

Giulio da Urbino, *Allegory of the Sack of Rome*

TWENTY-EIGHT

1527, END OF A WORLD

IT WAS A MASSACRE WITHOUT AN IMAGE. A horrible plunder that went on interminably and traumatized the entire Christian world. But Charles, Duke of Bourbon, commanding the imperial armies that captured Rome on May 6, 1527, arranged that there would be no images. It's hard today to conceive Europe's shock at the news that Rome had been sacked. And how can we understand the violence of the Lutheran Landsknechts except by acknowledging the depth of their resentment? This was the explanation offered by those in Charles V's entourage. Alfonso de Valdés, writing from Madrid, sang the requiem for the corrupt city to the following tune: "Each of the horrors of the sack of Rome is a precise, a necessary, a providential punishment for one of the shameful disgraces sullying the city."

Modern, disillusioned Europe bent its sorrowful attention in 1527 on the outstretched corpse of the city of Rome. News of the sack reached Florence on May 12. The shock was so great that it toppled the Medici regime. Four days later, a popular uprising called for the reinstatement of the Great Council. The Florentine Republic was restored, the same one that Machiavelli had so ardently defended, but also the one that he had patiently learned to detach himself from. Had his hour come around again? No, this time it really was too late. Niccolò Machiavelli offered his services, naturally, but the new regime gave preference to a former adherent of the Medici who had been quick to change his allegiance, rather than trust a man who had proved unfaithful to his republican ideals. Such is the world, which always gives preference to treachery over lucidity.

So it was over, and Machiavelli knew it. He had no doubt been preparing himself for death for some time. Here is a letter from his son Piero, thirteen, to his uncle, dated June 21, 1527:

> Dearest Francesco, I cannot hold back my tears in telling you that Niccolò, our father, died on the twenty-first of this month from stomach pains, which he developed after taking medication on the twentieth. He asked to confess his sins to Friar Matteo, who remained at his side until his death.

Confess his sins? That's not the image posterity retained. The story soon circulated that Machiavelli had had a dream before dying. A horde of ragged, miserable wretches were coming toward him. From the other direction came a solemn, noble assembly. He asked the first who they were: we are the saints, bound for paradise. The second group declared: we are the damned, going to hell. He recognized them then, for in their midst were all the great minds of antiquity, who had been so generous with him in conversation. In their company, he could continue to talk of politics. Why consign himself to boredom among the indigent? The choice was obvious: Machiavelli would follow the great men to hell.

This anecdote, of which the anti-Machiavellians made great use, could just possibly be true. When he died, surrounded by his friends, Machiavelli put the finishing touches on his portrait as a wicked provocateur. A reader of Lucretius who nonetheless took confession before dying, Machiavelli never explicitly spoke of his religious sentiments. What we do have is the image of himself he wanted to project in 1527 when the Christian world was teetering on the brink. History would continue without him, with him, against him — a history of ghosts and betrayals.

Tomb of Machiavelli, designed by Innocento Spinazzi

TWENTY-NINE

ANATOMY OF A GHOST

"NO EULOGY DOES JUSTICE TO SO GREAT A NAME." That is the epitaph engraved on Machiavelli's monument, paid for by public subscription in 1787, in the Church of Santa Croce in Florence. He was buried there on the day after his death, on June 22, 1527. But a writer's body is above all the body of his work. That is what haunts our modern political life, despite the indignation and the scandals, long after his death.

In August 1531, Pope Clement VII authorized the Roman printer Antonio Blado to publish Machiavelli's works: *The Prince*, the *Discourses*, and the *History of Florence*, in three volumes. Other editions followed shortly, in Florence and especially in Venice, which was then the publishing capital of Europe. The rhythm of publication and the books' affordable format suggest that the works found a ready market, despite having been written, according to the English cardinal Reginald Pole, "by the finger of Satan."

The times, in fact, were changing, and the distribution of Machiavelli's works soon came into conflict with the strict morals of the Counter-Reformation. The Jesuits orchestrated what amounted to an anti-Machiavellian campaign in Italy, and in 1559 *The Prince* and Machiavelli's other works were placed on the *Index Librorum Prohibitorum*. The *Index* was a list of pernicious books that one committed a mortal sin in reading — a list regularly updated by the Sacred Congregation of the Index until 1961. In theory it prohibited even quoting from the books in question. In Spain, where translations of *The Prince* quickly appeared, papal censure kept the book from being distributed. In France, on the other hand, it gave the work a boost: in the convoluted context of the Wars of Religion, Catherine de' Medici showed such partiality to the translation of *The Prince* by Jacques Gohory that the Huguenots didn't hesitate to brand her as Machiavellian.

While Machiavelli's name was being turned into an "-ism" — Machiavellianism was the worst insult that the high-minded could hurl at politicians — Machiavelli's ideas continued to circulate, but under borrowed names. Whenever an author from the sixteenth or seventeenth century made a reference to Tacitus, it was usually a winking allusion to Niccolò Machiavelli. Was this a question of veiling one's reference or of duping one's reader?

It almost seems that even during his lifetime, Machiavelli had started to disappear or at least to break up. In 1523, he was disagreeably surprised to learn that a respectable Aristotelian philosopher in Naples, Agostino Nifo, was passing off a pirated Latin translation of *The Prince* as his own — in a version that subverted the book's key concepts to exalt monarchy. After Machiavelli's death, his work continued to slowly break apart, eventually becoming as invisible as a mist.

A ghost, a lingering ghost. Not something we will ever move beyond. With him, according to him, against him, right up against him. But never without him.

Stefano Ussi, *Niccolò Machiavelli in His Study*

THIRTY

PHILOSOPHIZING IN A STORM

IT IS 1795, the end of the French Revolution, and Marc-Antoine Jullien is reading Machiavelli. He had been a member of the National Convention, a friend of Robespierre, and was arrested after the events of Thermidor. Now he has had a year to think about his downfall. "Read the sublime Machiavelli," he writes to one of his friends, "and you'll find the theory of our revolution and a history of the errors made by its participants, whom the revolution devoured."

It is 1864, and Maurice Joly is reading Machiavelli. Dismayed at the authoritarian empire of Napoleon III, he writes his *Dialogue in Hell Between Machiavelli and Montesquieu*. The former assails the latter with his implacable logic. He speaks in the enemy's voice. Montesquieu is a democrat, but his cause is hopeless. Matched against Machiavelli, the Enlightenment philosopher proves to be a man of the past.

It is 1933, and Antonio Gramsci is reading Machiavelli. A philosopher and a founding member of Italy's Communist Party, he has been in prison since a fascist prosecutor spoke at his trial, saying: "We must keep this brain from functioning for twenty years." Gramsci wants to know why republicanism failed along with "every attempt to create a collective, nationalist-populist movement." Much later, in 1972, the philosopher Louis Althusser commented: "If Machiavelli spoke to Gramsci, it wasn't in the past tense but in the present: better yet, the future."

It is 2020, and we are reading Machiavelli. Like all the others before us, we are reading him in the future tense. I emphasize all the others, because it wasn't just Jullien, Joly, and Gramsci who read him. When Gramsci read Machiavelli, it was in part to wrest him from the murderous clutches of Mussolini, who tried to make him the precursor of his new state, marked by the esthetic stylization of absolute power.

Everyone reads Machiavelli, losers and winners alike — even Silvio Berlusconi ventured to compose a preface to *The Prince*. So why put the spotlight on those who read Machiavelli to ward off disaster? In recognition of his unhappy fate? It's not just that. We also know that Machiavelli's name only comes up when a storm is threatening. He heralds tempests, not to avert them but to teach us to think in heavy weather.

Since his death in 1527, there have been many Machiavellian moments when his ideas have suddenly gained reality. By a Machiavellian moment, we should understand that precarious point when the ideal of republicanism has to confront its own powerlessness, the mutability of words and the opacity of representation, what we would call today the fatigue of democracy.

Raymond Aron said it in 1945: "The quarrel of Machiavellianism is rekindled every time a Caesar subjects Europe anew to servitude and war." Have we reached that point? Perhaps not, or at least not yet. If history is rife with Machiavellian moments, some are pronounced and some are less so — more discreet, insidious, stubborn. The less pronounced moments are not always the least perilous, particularly when accompanied by a general lethargy. Machiavelli is an awakener, because he is a writer. He writes to scratch his pen in the open wound. He writes not to revive the splendor of words but to say the truth about things.

READING MACHIAVELLI

THE MOST AUTHORITATIVE EDITIONS of the complete works of Machiavelli originate in Italy, and among the most reliable are the versions edited by Mario Martelli, *Tutte le opere* (Florence: Sansoni, 1971) and Corrado Vivanti, *Opere*, 3 vols. (Turin: Einaudi, 1997–2005), as well as the so-called national edition issued by Salerno Editrice, Rome, starting in 2000, which notably includes much of Machiavelli's diplomatic writing and his chancery correspondence before the Medici coup d'état in 1512. The publication of this enormous mass of texts, *Legazioni, Commissarie, Scritti di governo (1498–1512)*, 7 vols. (Rome: Salerno Editrice, 2001–2012), has revolutionized our understanding of Machiavelli in his primary role as a man of action.

In choosing a French translation of the principal works of Machiavelli, the reader may find the Bibliothèque de la Pléiade edition (1952) somewhat dated — though still valuable for the extraordinarily stimulating introduction by Jean Giono — and prefer the version edited by Christian Bec, *Œuvres* (Paris: Robert Laffont, 1996). That is the edition I have mainly used here, making only a very few corrections, but when it came to the *Discourses on the First Ten Books of Titus Livius*, I relied primarily on the excellent edition by Alessandro Fontana and Xavier Tabet, published by Gallimard in 2003.

There exist several recent translations of *The Prince* into French, all of them very useful. I edited an annotated and illustrated edition of this "nasty opuscule," *Le Prince* (Paris: Nouveau Monde, 2012), attempting to put the text in dialogue with the visual culture of the time, using illustrations chosen and captioned by Antonella Fenech-Kroke. We chose the alert, spoken-word translation by Jacqueline Risset, who captures Machiavelli's rapid-fire delivery perfectly. It was first published in 2001 by Actes Sud, based on a text prepared by Risset (one of the great translators of Dante) for a performance at the Théâtre des Amandiers in Nanterre in April 2001.

The translation I have used for this book is the more rigorous version by Jean-Louis Fournel and Jean-Claude Zancarini, published by Presses Universitaires de France in 2000 in an admirable critical edition: *De principatibus / Le Prince* (revised and corrected in 2014 for the "Quadrige" collection). That translation is inseparable from the learned commentary given by these two specialists in political philology, a commentary on which I have relied in many instances.

In 2013, the five hundredth anniversary of the writing of *The Prince* gave occasion to a number of scientific and publishing ventures, both in Italy and in Europe generally. The most notable was perhaps the publication by the Treccani Foundation of a three-volume *Enciclopedia machiavelliana*, edited by Genaro Sasso and Giorgio Inglese. Although the benchmark biography is still Roberto Ridolfi's two-volume *Vita di Niccolò Machiavelli*, published in 1954 and reissued several times since in revised editions, there exist highly recommendable biographies in French as well. Ugo Dotti's *La révolution Machiavel* (Grenoble: Jérôme Millon, 2006), originally published in 2003, is still valuable for its circumstantial account of Machiavelli's life, which is more briefly set forth in Marina Marietti's *Machiavel. Le penseur de la nécessité* (Paris: Payot, 2009). A lively and quick-paced account is given in Quentin Skinner's *Machiavelli: A Very Short Introduction* (New York: Oxford University Press, 1981; reissued 1996), usefully supplemented by Sandro Landi's very stimulating *Machiavel* (Paris: Ellipses, 2008).

To learn about the overall Italian context, it is well worth reading Élisabeth Crouzet-Pavan's *Renaissances italiennes, 1380–1500* (Paris: Albin Michel, 2007; reissued 2013), on which I drew, among other things, for the description of the tournament in Florence in 1469. For an introduction to the history of Florence under the Medici, one may consult the articles gathered in the special feature of *L'Histoire*, no. 274, March 2003, "La Florence des Médicis." The overall view of the system of Italian states during the fifteenth century and of the inventiveness of their forms of government that I have proposed here is more fully developed in "Les laboratoires politiques de l'Italie," in Patrick Boucheron, ed., *Histoire du monde au XVe siècle* (Paris: Fayard, 2009), pages 53–72.

I deliberately chose not to weigh down the text with references to the scholarly works that inspired it, yet certain allusions need all the same to be made more explicit here. Did the Renaissance spring full-blown from the rediscovery of Lucretius? This is the thesis that Stephen Greenblatt proposes in his brilliant and riveting *The Swerve* (New York and London: W. W. Norton, 2011). My comments on it in Chapter 5 fall in line with the skeptical reading given the book by Aurélien Robert in "Lucrèce et modernité" on the website *La vie des idées*. On the subject of Savonarola's prophesying (Chapter 6), I draw mainly on the hypotheses put forth in Jean-Louis Fournel and Jean-Claude Zancarini, *La politique de l'expérience. Savonarole, Guicciardini et le républicanisme florentin* (Turin: Edizioni dell'Orso, 2002); and our knowledge of the *Ricordanze* (Chapter 7) owes practically everything to Christiane Klapisch-Zuber's magnificent *La maison et le nom. Stratégies et rituels dans l'Italie de la Renaissance* (Paris: Éditions de l'EHESS, 1990). On Machiavelli's work in the chancery and its effect on his language (Chapter 9), I am indebted to the analyses collected in Jean-Jacques Marchand, ed., *Machiavello senza i Medici (1498–1512). Scrittura del potere / potere della scrittura* (Rome: Salerno, 2006). On Machiavelli's writing in general, my debt is to Harvey C. Mansfield, *Machiavelli's Virtue* (Chicago: The University of Chicago Press, 1996). As to the account of the events of 1527 (Chapter 28), it inevitably draws on the great work by André Chastel, *The Sack of Rome, 1527* (translated by Beth Archer [The A. W. Mellon Lectures in the Fine Arts, 1977; Bollingen Series XXXV: 26], Princeton-London: Princeton University Press, 1983).

Some of the themes discussed in this work I have addressed before, and I take the license to refer the reader to these earlier publications (and their relevant bibliographies). See for example, in relation to Chapter 10, but also on the question of the indeterminacy of politics and my reflections on *mésentente* (misunderstanding) in the sense given it by Jacques Rancière (whose influence pervades this book), my "Théories et pratiques du coup d'État dans l'Italie princière du *Quattrocento*," in François Foronda, Jean-Philippe Genet, and José Maria Nieto Soria, eds., *Coups d'État à la fin du Moyen Âge? Aux fondements du pouvoir politique en Europe occidentale* (Madrid, Collection de la Çasa de Velàzquez [91], 2005), pages 19–49.

The question of point of view, in the sense given it by Georges Didi-Huberman (for example, in his *The Eye of History: When Images Take Positions* (translated by Shane B. Lillis, RIC BOOKS [Ryerson Image Centre Books], The MIT Press, 2018), inspired my thinking on "the political art of taking a position" (Chapter 20), which was initially developed in my *Léonard et Machiavel* (Lagrasse: Verdier, 2009). In the context of my reflections on fate and the river (Chapter 15), which also touch on the relation between political defeat and ideological lucidity, see the treatment given these topics in my *L'entretemps* (Lagrasse: Verdier, 2012), especially pages

110 et seq. Finally, Machiavelli's letter to his friend Francesco Vettori in 1513 (Chapter 11), which has been the subject of such ample commentary, received a fuller treatment in my *Au banquet des savoirs. Éloge dantesque de la transmission* (Bordeaux-Pau: Presses universitaires de Bordeaux / Presses universitaires de Pau et des Pays de l'Adour, 2015).

My appreciation of *The Prince* in Chapters 11–15 builds on a multitude of works but, aside from the critical editions already mentioned, owes a particular debt to the studies gathered by Yves-Charles Zarka and Thierry Ménissier in *Machiavel, Le Prince ou le nouvel art politique* (Paris: Presses Universitaires de France, 2001) and, in a more general way, to Marie Gaille, *Machiavel et la tradition philosophique* (Paris: Presses Universitaires de France, 2007). It isn't possible, as the reader will have realized, to read Machiavelli without at the same time reading all those who, in good faith or bad, have leaned over his shoulder to ponder him, annotate him, criticize him. See on this score Paolo Carta and Xavier Tabat, eds., *Machiavelli nel XIX e nel XX secolo / Machiavel aux XIXe et XXe siècles* (Padua: CEDAM, 2007). I have borrowed from this book the quotation from Marc-Antoine Jullien; the extract from Maurice Joly comes from Carlo Ginzburg's "Representing the Enemy: On the French Prehistory of the *Protocols*," in Carlo Ginzburg, tr. Anne C. Tedeschi and John Tedeschi, *Threads and Traces: True, False, Fictive* (Berkeley and Los Angeles: University of California Press, 2012). See also Giuseppe Ferrari, *Machiavel, juge des révolutions de notre temps* (Paris: Fayot, 2003), original edition 1849; Louis Althusser, ed. François Matheron, *Écrits philosophiques et politiques* (Paris: Stock / IMEC, 1995), quotation page 51 on Gramsci reading Machiavelli.

The term "Machiavellian moment" has been used — ever since John G. A. Pocock's celebrated *The Machiavellian Moment: Florentine Political Thought and the Atlantic Republican Tradition* (Princeton, N.J.: Princeton University Press, 2016), original edition 1975 — to describe the dawning realization of the inadequacy of the republican ideal. Taking account of the criticisms the concept has drawn (notably in Gérald Sfez and Michel Sennelart, *L'enjeu Machiavel* [Paris: Presses Universitaires de France, 2004]), I see it more broadly as the brutal and disillusioned reappearance of Machiavellian thought whenever the evidence of political indecision surfaces. In that context, the interpretation presented here owes much to the work of Claude Lefort, *Machiavelli in the Making* (translated by Michael B. Smith [Studies in Phenomenology and Existential Philosophy], Northwestern University Press, 2012), and *Writing: The Political Test* (translated by David Ames Curtis [Post-Contemporary Interventions], Duke University Press, 2000), and perhaps even more to the few but sumptuous pages of Maurice Merleau-Ponty's "A Note on Machiavelli," in *Signs* (translated by Richard C. McCleary [Studies in Phenomenology and Existential Philosophy], Northwestern University Press, 1964), pages 211–223. It is those pages that drive this book's introduction.

IMAGE CREDITS

p. viii Illustration by Tim O'Brien, from *Time*. Copyright
© 2017 TIME USA LLC. All rights reserved. Used
under license.

p. 12 Fresco by Giovanni Stradano (1523–1605), under
the direction of Giorgio Vasari. Raffaello Bencini /
Alinari Archives, Florence

p. 14 Painting by Sandro Botticelli, circa 1480. Uffizi
Gallery, Florence. colaimages / Alamy Stock Photo

p. 18 Painting by Santi di Tito (1536–1603). Palazzo
Vecchio, Florence. GL Archive / Alamy Stock Photo

p. 22 Painting by Peter Paul Rubens, circa 1612–1616.
Museum Plantin-Moretus, Antwerp, Belgium.

p. 26 Photograph by Giuseppe Alinari, circa 1857. The
Miriam and Ira D. Wallach Division of Art,
Prints and Photographs: Photography Collection,
The New York Public Library.

p. 29 Photograph by Giuseppe Alinari, circa 1850s. The
Miriam and Ira D. Wallach Division of Art,
Prints and Photographs: Photography Collection,
The New York Public Library.

p. 30 Title page of 1563 edition. OLC.L964.563, Houghton Library, Harvard University.

p. 35 Photograph by Joseph Vigier, 1853. Gilman Collection, Gift of The Howard Gilman Foundation, 2005.

p. 36 Illuminated painting by Jean Bourdichon, circa 1507, one of eleven miniatures in *Le Voyage de Gênes* by Jean Marot. Bibliothèque nationale de France. World History Archive / Alamy Stock Photo

p. 38 Painting by Fra Bartolomeo, circa 1498. Museo Nazionale di San Marco, Florence. Azoor Photo / Alamy Stock Photo

p. 41 Woodcut by unknown artist, circa 1498. Rosenwald Collection, Rare Book and Special Collections Division, Library of Congress.

p. 42 Painting after Francesco Rosselli, 1498. Museo Nazionale di San Marco, Florence. Azoor Photo Collection / Alamy Stock Photo

p. 45 Film still from *Zero for Conduct*, directed by Jean Vigo, 1933.

p. 46 Painting from the workshop of Jean Perréal, circa 1514. Private collection. Matthew Corrigan / Alamy Stock Photo

p. 50 Document, 1508. By permission of the Ministry of Cultural Heritage and Activities / Central National Library Florence

p. 53 Photograph by Giuseppe Alinari, circa 1850s. The Miriam and Ira D. Wallach Division of Art, Prints and Photographs: Photography Collection, The New York Public Library.

p. 54   Painting by Ridolfo del Ghirlandaio, 16th century.
         Private collection. The Picture Art Collection /
         Alamy Stock Photo

p. 57   Photograph by Lourens Smak, 2006. Lourens Smak /
         Alamy Stock Photo

p. 58   Photograph by dan74, 2010. dan74 / Alamy Stock Photo

p. 60   Letter, 1513. By permission of the Ministry of
         Cultural Heritage and Activities / Central National
         Library Florence

p. 64   Ink on paper, 16th century. Bibliothèque nationale
         de France.

p. 68   Penguin Classics book cover featuring a detail from
         Charles IX of France, a painting by Francois Couet, 1563.
         Musée du Louvre. Photograph © Barney Burstein /
         Corbis Historical via Getty Images. Book cover
         copyright © Penguin Books, 2011. Translation and
         editorial material copyright © Tim Parks, 2009.

p. 72   Illuminated painting by Gherardo del Fora, circa 1480.
         Spencer Collection, The New York Public Library.

p. 75   Film still from *Ivan the Terrible*, directed by Sergei
         Eisenstein, 1944.

p. 77   Published by W. W. Norton & Company, New York,
         1968, reissued in 1999.

p. 79   Ink drawing on paper by Leonardo da Vinci, 1473. Uffizi
         Galleries, Florence. Art Heritage / Alamy Stock Photo

p. 80   Pen and ink drawing on paper by Leonardo da Vinci,
         1504. Windsor Castle, The Royal Library. Copyright ©
         DEA Picture Library / De Agostini Editore / AGE
         Fotostock

158

p. 120   Etching and engraving by Antoinette Bouzonnet-Stella, after Antoine Bouzonnet-Stella, 1677. The Miriam and Ira D. Wallach Division of Art, Prints and Photographs: Print Collection, The New York Public Library.

p. 124   Painting by Giuseppe Lorenzo Gatteri (1829–1884). Municipality of Trieste. Department of Education, Tourism Promotion, Culture and Sport. Museum and Library Services.

p. 126   Painting by Sebastiano del Piombo, 1531. The Getty Museum. Digital image courtesy of the Getty's Open Content Program.

p. 130   Photograph by Cola Images, 2016. colaimages / Alamy Stock Photo

p. 134   Maiolica dish by Giulio da Urbino, 1534. The British Museum. Copyright © The Trustees of the British Museum. All rights reserved.

p. 138   Marble tomb by Innocenzo Spinazzi, 1787. Basilica of Santa Croce, Florence. Peter Barritt / Alamy Stock Photo

p. 142   Painting by Stefano Ussi, 1894. Galleria Nazionale d'Arte Moderna e Contemporanea, Rome. The Picture Art Collection / Alamy Stock Photo

The author would like to thank Adrien Genoudet
for his work in researching and selecting the illustrations.

PATRICK BOUCHERON is a French historian. He previously taught medieval history at the École normale supérieure and the University of Paris, and is currently a professor of history at the Collège de France. He is the author of twelve books and the editor of five, including *France in the World*, which became a bestseller.

WILLARD WOOD has translated more than twenty-five books from French. He is a recipient of the Lewis Galantière Award for Literary Translation and a National Endowment for the Arts Fellowship in Translation. He lives in Norfolk, Connecticut.

Praise for
MACHIAVELLI

"An elegant introduction to this disturbing, incisive, many-sided thinker—and a reminder of why we must read him right now."

SARAH BAKEWELL, AUTHOR OF
HOW TO LIVE: A LIFE OF MONTAIGNE

"An energetic new book by Patrick Boucheron offers a knowing guide to the Renaissance statesman and writer's life and work."

NEW YORK TIMES BOOK REVIEW, EDITORS' CHOICE

"Packed with insights into how Machiavelli has been construed and misconstrued down the ages and why his ideas still resonate so powerfully today... Boucheron's book...reminds us that Machiavelli is no advocate of unbridled state violence."

FINANCIAL TIMES

"'When a storm is threatening' and our institutions are in crisis, Boucheron concludes his book, Machiavelli can 'teach us to think in heavy weather.'... Machiavelli no doubt would have been fascinated by Trump, but even more so by the circumstances and society that allowed him to be successful."

NEW YORK REVIEW OF BOOKS

"In a slim, beautifully illustrated volume, French
historian Boucheron…distills the life and works
of Renaissance writer Niccolò Machiavelli…
A penetrating portrait of a complex political thinker."

KIRKUS REVIEWS

"[Boucheron] ground[s] this concise study not in
abstruse theory but in his subject's biography,
his life's work, and the contingencies of
Florentine political history…While many imagine
the author of *The Prince* as a fork-tongued whisperer,
Boucheron makes the case for him as
more a clear-eyed critic, writing for the many
rather than the few, leaving behind a guide
for disillusionment in murky times such as our own."

NEW CRITERION

"As part of his view of a self-aware and socially engaged
history, Boucheron offers a Machiavelli who is
a 'scout': someone able to think from uncharted
and dangerous territory, and thus someone who needs
to be read 'not in the present but in the future tense.'
Boucheron's forward-looking analysis is anchored in
the past—in his studies of the relation between
political power and urban transformations
in medieval Milan—and aimed at broadening
the limits of historical interpretation."

BOSTON REVIEW

"*Machiavelli* provide[s] a distinct perspective on
the influential philosopher…Readers looking to learn
more about the thinker, as well as those seeking
an introduction, will find this creative work appealing."

LIBRARY JOURNAL

"Patrick Boucheron gives us a trenchant analysis
of Machiavelli's complex and slippery ideas. Even more
useful and illuminating, with Machiavelli as his guide,
he probes our own political life and times. In an age
of shrill and often senseless debate, it's a pleasure to read
such a subtle and gently provoking thinker."

ROSS KING, AUTHOR OF
MACHIAVELLI: PHILOSOPHER OF POWER

"Machiavelli is the antidote we need to today's delusion
that reality can be virtual or augmented—that is,
easily doctored by us ourselves or the media.
Reading him now is necessary, more than ever before.
But who reads him? Patrick Boucheron's little book is
by far the best inducement to Machiavelli that I know of,
to the point that I will have students read
Boucheron's *Machiavelli* rather than Machiavelli's
Prince in my surveys. I am sure that they will then get to
The Prince, and not for class, but for themselves."

FRANCESCO ERSPAMER, PROFESSOR OF ROMANCE LANGUAGES
AND LITERATURES, HARVARD UNIVERSITY, AND DIRECTOR OF
THE HARVARD SUMMER PROGRAM IN MILAN AND SIENA